Economic Perspectives

NIPA® GENX ELECTRONIC RESOURCES & SOLUTIONS P. LTD.
New Delhi-110 034

About the Editors

Dr. Supriya is presently working as Assistant Professor in the Department of Agricultural Economics Acharya Narendra Deva University of Agriculture and Technology, Ayodhya (U.P.) She has completed her Doctorate Degree in Agricultural Economics from G. B. P.U A & T, Pantnagar in year 2009 and qualified ARS Net in Economics and Agribusiness Management. She has also done Post Graduate Diploma in Business Management with Human Resources as specialization from SCDL, Pune and M.A. Economics from Kumaon University. She has received University Fellowship during Master's and Doctoral Program.

She has varied experience in the fields of research and teaching while working at IARI, New Delhi and Teaching at G.B.P.U.A&T, Pantnagar.

She has more than 50 Research articles published in reputed NAAS rated and other peer reviewed journals. She wrote Book on "Farm Management and its Practical Utility", "Agribusiness Fundamentals of Decision Making" and "Manual Cum Workbook on Agricultural Finance & Cooperation". In collaboration with Extension and Statistics Fellows also contributed Book chapters and book in the area of Extension Education and Agricultural Statistics. She has also written many popular articles published in Hindi and English Magazines. She has also received Excellence awards by many societies in the area of Research and Teaching like Young Scientist award and Excellence in Teaching. She has taught various courses at Undergraduate and Post Graduate level. Her area of specialization is Agricultural Economics with Agricultural statistics as minor.

Dr. Pradeep Mishra, is an Assistant Professor of Statistics at the College of Agriculture, Rewa at the Jawaharlal Nehru Krishi Vishwa Vidyalaya, Madhya Pradesh, India. During his PhD research work, he was selected for an INSPIRE Fellowship by the Department of Science and Technology of the Government of India. Dr. Mishra has served as a data management specialist at a private multinational company for several years. His area of specialization is agriculture statistics, time series, and design of experiment. He has published more than 68 research articles in different international and national journals. Also, he won several awards, including an award for young scientists in at an international conference (GRISAAS-2017); best doctoral degree in 2018 at an international conference on advances in agriculture and allied science technologies for sustainable development, in Hyderabad, a second best paper award from the Society of Economics & Development in PAU. 2018, among others. Dr. Mishra earned his BSc in Agriculture from the College of Agriculture, Bilaspur, affiliated with the Indira Gandhi Krishi Vishwavidyalaya, Raipur (C.G.); his MSc in Agricultural Statistics from the College of Agriculture, Jawaharlal Nehru Agricultural University; and his PhD in Agriculture Statistics, specializing in modeling and forecasting of foods crops in India and their yield sustainability.

Prateek Kumar is presently pursuing Ph.D. in the Department of Extension Education, Acharya Narendra Deva University of Agriculture & Technology, Kumarganj, Ayodhya (U.P.). He has completed his Master's degree from Bundelkhand University, Jhansi in 2022. He has done research work on Green fodder under the supervision of IGFRI scientist. He has published research papers published in peer reviewed National and International journal. He wrote 5 popular articles and 8 book Chapters. He has also received Young Scientist Award.

Economic Perspectives
Navigating the Financial Landscape

Supriya
Assistant Professor
Department of Agricultural Economics
Acharya Narendra Deva University of Agriculture and Technology
Kumarganj, Ayodhya, Uttar Pradesh

Pradeep Mishra
Assistant Professor
Department of Agricultural Statistics
College of Agriculture, Rewa
Jawaharlal Nehru Krishi Vishwavidyalaya
Jabalpur, Madhya Pradesh

Prateek Kumar
Research Scholar
Department of Extension Education
Acharya Narendra Deva University of Agriculture and Technology
Kumarganj, Ayodhya, Uttar Pradesh

NIPA® GENX ELECTRONIC RESOURCES & SOLUTIONS P. LTD.
New Delhi-110 034

NIPA® GENX ELECTRONIC RESOURCES & SOLUTIONS P. LTD.

101,103, Vikas Surya Plaza, CU Block
L.S.C.Market, Pitam Pura, New Delhi-110 034
Ph : +91 11 27341616, 27341717, 27341718
E-mail: newindiapublishingagency@gmail.com
www: www.nipabooks.com

For customer assistance, please contact
Phone: + 91-11-27 34 17 17
Fax: + 91-11-27 34 16 16

Print ISBN: 978-93-58878-81-3
ebook ISBN: 978-93-58874-80-8

Composed and Designed by NIPA®.

Preface

This book delves into the intricate world of economics, offering a comprehensive exploration of the diverse perspectives that shape our understanding of the financial landscape.

In today's rapidly evolving global economy, having a nuanced understanding of economic principles is more crucial than ever. This book aims to provide readers with a holistic view of various economic theories, models, and real-world applications, equipping them with the knowledge needed to navigate the complexities of the financial world.

Through a collection of insightful chapters written by esteemed experts in the field, this book covers a wide range of topics, from macroeconomic trends to microeconomic analysis, from financial markets to policy implications. Each chapter offers a unique perspective, contributing to a rich tapestry of economic insights that will broaden your understanding of the forces at play in the financial landscape.

Whether you are a student, a professional economist, a policymaker, or simply a curious reader interested in economics, "Economic Perspectives: Navigating the Financial Landscape" promises to be a valuable resource that will inform, inspire, and provoke thought.

I extend my heartfelt gratitude to the contributors who have shared their expertise and insights in this book, as well as to the editorial team whose dedication and hard work have brought this project to fruition. It is my hope that this book will serve as a beacon of knowledge and a catalyst for deeper exploration into the fascinating world of economics.

I invite you to embark on this intellectual journey with us, as we navigate the financial landscape together and uncover the diverse economic perspectives that shape our world.

Editors

Contents

Preface vii

1. **Unveiling the Mysteries of MSP: A Comprehensive Analysis 1**
   Brijesh Kumar Gupta and Abhishek Kalia

2. **Financial Markets: The Lifeline of Economies 15**
   Harshit Mishra, Divyanshi Mishra and Manaswini, N.

3. **Dynamics of Agricultural Economics and Minimum Support Prices 29**
   Sandeep Gautam, Shiv Kumar Rana, Abhishek Raj Ranjan

4. **Economic Reforms: Liberalization Privatization and Globalization...37**
   Yellagandula Mani and Mahima Priyanka Neerugatti

5. **The Interplay Between Minimum Support Price (MSP) and Market Forces...53**
   Narendra Yadav and Diksha Bohra

6. **Deciphering Economic Policies: Fiscal Measures and Beyond......63**
   Harshit Mishra, Ankit Tiwari and Deepchand Nishad

7. **Public Finance: Expenditure, Revenue and Debt Dynamics 77**
   Shweta Chaudhary and Ruch Rani Gangwar

8. **Banking on Growth: The Role of Finance in Development 87**
   Km Deepshikha, Monmath Gopal and Sachin Kumar Verma

9. **Global Finance: Understanding International Monetary System 99**
   Monmath Gopal, Km Deepshikha and Ankit Kumar Shakya

10. **Monetary Policy: Steering The Economic Ship............................111**
    Deep Narayan Yadav, Ankit Kumar Shakya, Ankit Tiwari and Manaswini, N.

11. The Future of Finance: Trends, Predictions, and Preparations..125
Shiv Kumar Rana, Sandeep Gautam and Prateek Kumar

12. Understanding Economics Cycle: Recession Recovery and Beyond 133

Mahima Priyanka Neerugatti, Aditya Bhooshan Srivastava Sachin Kumar Verma and Deep Chand Nishad

13. The Economics of Subsidies: Balancing Support and Sustainability..141
Diksha Bohra, Narendra Yadav and Aakash Mhaskey

Index..**149**

1

Unveiling the Mysteries of MSP A Comprehensive Analysis

Brijesh Kumar Gupta[1] and Abhishek Kalia[2*]

[1]Department of Agricultural Extension, Banda University of Agriculture and Technology, Banda, Uttar Pradesh

[2]Department of Basic and Social Sciences, Banda University of Agriculture and Technology, Banda, Uttar Pradesh

Abstract

The Minimum Support Price (MSP) is a major policy tool in India aiming to ensure farmers receive a minimum price for their crops. Announced by the government before sowing seasons, MSP acts as a safety net against price crashes. However, the policy sparks debate on its effectiveness and impact. MSPs consider production costs, demand-supply and global market trends. While aiming to incentivize production and ensure farmer income, critics argue political considerations can influence MSP levels. Proponents highlight MSP's role in supporting farmers' income and ensuring food security. However, concerns exist about potential distortions. MSPs for certain crops might encourage monoculture and discourage diversification. Additionally, market dynamics can be disrupted if market prices consistently fall below MSP, leading to government procurement challenges and storage burdens. The effectiveness of MSP in achieving its objectives is a subject of ongoing debate. Discussions centre on improving targeting mechanisms to ensure benefits reach vulnerable farmers, while also exploring alternative support systems like crop insurance and direct income transfers. Long-term reforms might involve gradual transitions towards market-oriented policies with efficient price discovery mechanisms.

Keywords: *Farmers, Income, Market, Minimum Support Price (MSP), Price*

Introduction

Agriculture forms the bedrock of the Indian economy, employing over half of the country's workforce and contributing significantly to its GDP. Despite the rise of other sectors, agriculture remains vital for ensuring national food security and the livelihood of millions of farmers. However, Indian farmers face several challenges, including volatile market prices, unpredictable weather patterns and high input costs (Chintapalli and Tang, 2021). In this context, the MSP scheme emerges as a crucial government intervention aimed at safeguarding farmers' incomes and promoting agricultural stability. According to the latest data from the Ministry of Agriculture and Farmers Welfare, the agricultural sector contributes around 15-18% to India's GDP. While this share has decreased somewhat with the expansion of other sectors, agriculture still sustains the livelihoods of over 54% of the workforce, primarily concentrated in rural areas. Furthermore, India ranks as a leading producer of various agricultural commodities, including pulses, cotton, milk, and rice. This highlights the sector's critical role in ensuring domestic food supplies and contributing to global food security (Mahto and Patil, 2023).

Despite its significance, Indian agriculture faces several challenges. One of the most significant concerns is price volatility. Agricultural produce is often subject to fluctuations in market prices, leaving farmers vulnerable to distress sales during periods of surplus production. Additionally, unpredictable weather patterns due to climate change can significantly impact crop yields, leading to income losses for farmers. Furthermore, the rising costs of essential inputs like fertilizers, pesticides and seeds put a strain on farmers' profit margins (Aditya *et al.,* 2017). These factors combined create a situation of uncertainty and economic hardship for a vast section of the rural population. The MSP scheme was introduced by the Government of India in the 1960s as a critical policy intervention to address the challenges faced by farmers. MSP acts as a floor price for certain agricultural commodities, below which the government guarantees to procure produce from farmers at pre-determined prices. This mechanism aims to provide a safety net for farmers, ensuring they receive a minimum return on their investment even during periods of low market prices.

The MSP for covered crops is determined by the Commission for Agricultural Costs and Prices (CACP), a government-appointed body. The CACP considers various factors while recommending MSPs, including the cost of production for farmers, prevailing market prices and a minimum profit margin to incentivize production. After considering the CACP's recommendations, the government announces MSPs for covered crops before the sowing season, allowing farmers to make informed decisions about their cropping patterns (Mahto and Patil, 2023; Prabha *et al.,* 2023). The MSP scheme serves multiple objectives that are vital for the health of the agricultural sector. Firstly, it aims to protect farmers from price fluctuations and ensure a minimum level of income for their produce. This not only safeguards their livelihoods but also incentivizes continued agricultural production. Secondly, MSP helps to maintain buffer stocks of essential food grains, contributing to national food security and enabling the government to implement welfare programs effectively. Finally, the MSP scheme encourages investment in agriculture by providing a measure of stability and predictability to farmers (Chintapalli and Tang, 2022).

While the MSP scheme holds significant value for Indian agriculture, it is not without its critics. Some argue that the current system of MSP procurement primarily benefits large, well-resourced farmers and overlooks small and marginal farmers who often struggle to access government procurement centres. Additionally, concerns exist regarding the financial sustainability of the scheme, with some suggesting that the government may struggle to continue procuring large quantities of produce at MSPs, particularly during years of surplus production. Furthermore, the MSP system can sometimes distort market forces, leading to inefficiencies in the agricultural value chain (Bhattarai and GC, 2020). The MSP scheme plays a critical role in supporting Indian agriculture and ensuring the well-being of farmers. By providing a safety net against price fluctuations and incentivizing production, MSP contributes to the stability and sustainability of the agricultural sector. However, ongoing debate and potential reforms are necessary to ensure the scheme's effectiveness and address concerns regarding its reach and long-term financial viability. As India strives to modernize its agricultural sector and improve farmers income, the MSP scheme will likely remain a key policy tool, requiring continuous evaluation and refinement to meet the evolving needs of the agricultural landscape (Visnu and Babu, 2023).

Foundations of Minimum Support Price

Economic Theory Behind Price Supports

a. **Market Failure and Market Distortions:** The concept of MSP finds its roots in economic theories related to market failure and market distortions. Market failure occurs when the free-market mechanism fails to allocate resources efficiently, leading to either underproduction or overproduction of goods. In agricultural markets, market failures are often prevalent due to factors such as imperfect competition, information asymmetry and externalities. These failures result in volatile prices that do not adequately reflect the costs of production, leading to income uncertainties for farmers. MSP aims to address these distortions by providing a floor price for agricultural commodities, thereby ensuring a stable income for farmers and mitigating the effects of market fluctuations.

b. **Price Floors vs. Price Ceilings:** Price supports, such as minimum support price, are often implemented through the establishment of price floors. A price floor is a minimum price set by the government or a regulatory authority above the equilibrium price determined by the market forces. This ensures that the market price does not fall below a certain level, protecting the interests of producers. Price floors differ from price ceilings, which are maximum prices set below the equilibrium to protect consumers from excessively high prices, as shown in Figure 1. MSP operates as a price floor, ensuring that farmers receive a fair return for their produce and preventing prices from falling below a predetermined level.

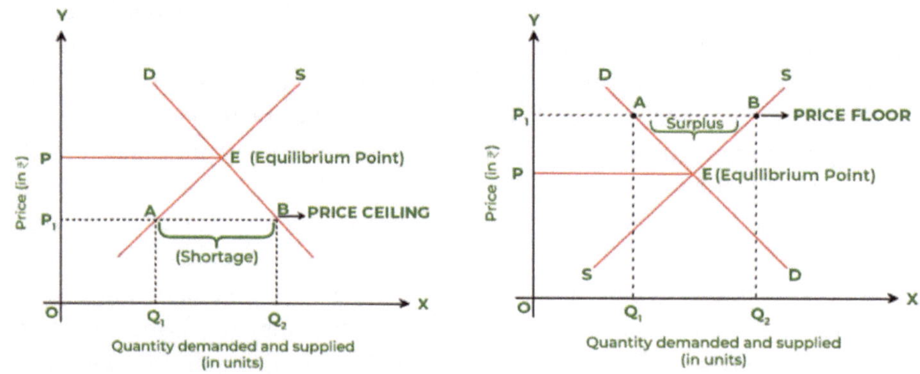

Fig. 1. Price Ceiling (in left) and Price Floor (in right)

Role of Government Intervention in Agricultural Markets

a. **Market Stabilization and Price Smoothing:** Government intervention in agricultural markets, such as the implementation of MSP policies, serves the dual purpose of market stabilization and price smoothing. By setting a floor price for agricultural commodities, governments aim to stabilize prices by preventing sharp declines during periods of surplus production. This intervention helps to maintain the financial viability of farmers by ensuring a minimum level of income even in adverse market conditions. Additionally, MSP policies contribute to price smoothing by reducing price volatility, which in turn promotes investment and risk management in the agricultural sector (Chintapalli and Tang, 2022).

b. **Income Support for Farmers:** One of the primary objectives of MSP policies is to provide income support for farmers. Agriculture is inherently risky, with farmers exposed to various uncertainties such as weather fluctuations, pest attacks and market price volatility. MSP guarantees a minimum level of income for farmers, thereby reducing their financial risk and ensuring livelihood security. This income support enables farmers to cover their production costs, invest in technology and inputs and sustain their agricultural activities even during periods of unfavourable market conditions.

Critiques and Debates Surrounding MSP Policies

a. **Efficiency vs. Equity Considerations:** Critics of MSP policies often raise concerns about their efficiency and equity implications. While MSPs provide income support for farmers and stabilize agricultural markets, they may also lead to inefficiencies by distorting resource allocation and promoting overproduction of certain crops. Moreover, MSPs tend to primarily benefit large landholding farmers, exacerbating income inequalities within the agricultural sector. Critics argue that alternative policy measures, such as income support schemes targeted towards small and marginalized farmers, may be more equitable and efficient in addressing the challenges faced by the agricultural community.

b. **Impact on Market Dynamics and Producer Behaviour:** The implementation of MSP policies can have significant implications for market dynamics and producer behaviour. By guaranteeing a minimum price for agricultural commodities, MSPs may discourage farmers from diversifying their crops or adopting innovative farming practices that could enhance productivity and sustainability. Moreover, MSPs may distort market signals by artificially inflating prices, leading to misallocation of resources and inefficiencies in the long run. Critics argue that reliance on MSPs may hinder the transition towards a more market-oriented agricultural system, thereby impeding the sector's competitiveness and resilience in the global marketplace.

The foundations of MSP encompass economic theories related to market failure, government intervention and price stabilization. While MSP policies play a crucial role in providing income support for farmers and stabilizing agricultural markets, they also face critiques regarding their efficiency, equity and long-term impact on market dynamics. A comprehensive analysis of MSP policies necessitates a nuanced understanding of these theoretical underpinnings and the complex dynamics of agricultural markets (Kumar and Mazhar, 2021).

Methodological Approaches to Analysing Minimum Support Price

MSP is a crucial policy tool in agricultural economics, aimed at ensuring price stability and income security for farmers. Analysing its effects requires robust methodological approaches that can capture the complex dynamics of agricultural markets. In this comprehensive analysis, we discuss the various methodological approaches used to study MSP and understand its implications.

Empirical Techniques for Evaluating MSP Effects

Empirical analysis forms the backbone of MSP research, employing various techniques to assess the impact of MSP on different economic outcomes.

a. **Econometric Models and Time-Series Analysis:** Econometric models, such as regression analysis, are commonly used to estimate the relationship between MSP and key variables like agricultural production, prices and farmer income. Time-series analysis allows researchers to track changes in these variables over time, identifying trends and assessing the effectiveness of MSP in achieving its objectives. By controlling for other factors that may influence outcomes, econometric models provide valuable insights into the causal effects of MSP.

b. **Comparative Statics and Counterfactual Analysis:** Comparative statics analysis compares outcomes before and after MSP interventions or between regions with and without MSP implementation. This approach helps isolate the effects of MSP from other factors affecting agricultural markets. Counterfactual analysis, including methods like difference-in-differences or propensity score matching, further refines this comparison by constructing a plausible scenario in the absence of MSP. By simulating what would have happened without MSP, researchers can estimate its true impact on farmers' welfare, market prices, and production decisions (Kumar *et al.*, 2021).

Data Sources and Challenges in MSP Research

The success of MSP analysis critically depends on the quality and availability of data, as well as addressing inherent challenges in agricultural data collection.

a. **Availability and Reliability of Price Data:** Access to accurate and reliable price data is essential for MSP research. However, agricultural markets are often characterized by fragmented information systems, making it challenging to obtain comprehensive price data. Moreover, MSP operations may not always be transparent, leading to discrepancies between official MSP prices and actual market prices. Researchers must carefully navigate these data challenges, relying on a combination of government reports, surveys, and market intelligence to construct reliable price series for analysis.

b. **Incorporating Non-Market Factors into Analysis:** MSP analysis must also consider non-market factors that influence agricultural outcomes, such as government policies, weather shocks and technological advancements. Ignoring these factors can lead to biased estimates of MSP effects. Researchers employ various strategies, such as instrumental variable techniques or panel data analysis, to account for these confounding factors and obtain more accurate estimates of MSP impacts.

Determinants of Minimum Support Price

MSP is a crucial aspect of agricultural policy, directly impacting farmers' income and food security. Understanding the determinants of MSP involves analysing various factors that influence its setting, as well as the political economy behind the decision-making process.

Factors Influencing MSP Setting

Setting the MSP involves considering several economic factors that affect agricultural production and market dynamics:

a. Production Costs and Input Prices

- **Cost of Production:** The MSP is often pegged to cover production costs, ensuring farmers receive remunerative prices for their produce. Factors such as labour costs, fertilizers, seeds, machinery and other inputs play a significant role.
- **Inflation:** Fluctuations in inflation rates directly impact input prices, influencing the MSP calculation. Higher inflation may necessitate a higher MSP to maintain farmers' real income.
- **Technological Changes:** Advancements in agricultural technology can affect production costs. For instance, the adoption of mechanization may reduce labour costs but increase capital investment.

b. International Market Prices and Trade Policies

- **Global Supply and Demand:** International market prices for agricultural commodities influence domestic MSPs, especially for crops with significant export-import dynamics.
- **Trade Policies:** Government policies regarding tariffs, subsidies and trade agreements can affect domestic prices. Import duties and export subsidies may be used to stabilize domestic prices relative to international markets.

Political Economy of MSP Decision-Making

In addition to economic factors, the determination of MSP is significantly influenced by the political dynamics surrounding agricultural policy:

a. Government Budgetary Constraints

- **Fiscal Policy:** Setting MSP involves budgetary allocations, which must be balanced with other expenditure priorities like infrastructure, social welfare, and defence.
- **Subsidies:** MSP operations often involve subsidies, which can strain government finances. Budget constraints may limit the extent to which MSPs can be increased without risking fiscal stability.

b. Interest Group Politics and Farmer Lobbying

- **Farmers' Organizations:** Strong farmer lobbies and interest groups advocate for higher MSPs to safeguard farmers' interests and ensure agricultural viability.
- **Political Parties:** MSP decisions are influenced by political considerations, especially in agrarian economies where farmers constitute a significant vote bank. Governments may adjust MSPs to garner political support.

Impacts of Minimum Support Price Policies

Effects on Producer Behaviour and Crop Choices

MSP policies have significant implications for the behaviour of agricultural producers and the choices they make regarding crop cultivation. This section explores two key aspects: crop diversification and monoculture trends and the contrast between intensive and extensive farming practices.

a. **Crop Diversification and Monoculture Trends:** MSP policies can influence farmers' decisions regarding which crops to cultivate. In many cases, MSPs are set for staple crops like wheat and rice, which may lead to an overemphasis on these crops at the expense of others. This can result in monoculture trends where farmers predominantly grow MSP-supported crops, leading to reduced biodiversity in agricultural landscapes. Conversely, if MSPs are extended to a wider range of crops, it may incentivize diversification, leading to a more resilient agricultural system.

b. **Intensive vs. Extensive Farming Practices:** The implementation of MSP policies can also impact farming practices in terms of intensity. When MSPs are set at levels perceived to be remunerative, farmers may adopt more intensive practices to maximize yields and profits. This could involve increased use of inputs such as fertilizers and pesticides, leading to concerns about environmental sustainability and long-term soil health. Conversely, if MSPs are not sufficiently supportive, farmers may resort to extensive farming methods, expanding land use to compensate for low returns per unit area (Janaiah and Shireesha, 2020).

Market Dynamics and Price Distortions

MSP policies can introduce distortions into agricultural markets, affecting supply-demand dynamics and creating spillover effects on both MSP-supported and non-supported crops as well as other sectors within the agricultural economy.

a. **Supply-Demand Dynamics in MSP-Subsidized Crops:** The establishment of MSPs can alter the traditional supply-demand dynamics in agricultural markets. By guaranteeing a minimum price for certain crops, MSPs can incentivize increased production, potentially leading to surpluses in years of high yields. This surplus may put downward pressure on prices, especially if storage and distribution infrastructure is inadequate to absorb excess production. Conversely, in years of poor harvests, MSPs can provide a safety net for farmers, stabilizing incomes and ensuring food security (Geetha and Mahesh, 2019).

b. **Spillover Effects on Non-MSP Crops and Agricultural Sectors:** The implementation of MSP policies can also have indirect effects on crops that are not covered by MSPs. If farmers perceive MSP-supported crops as more lucrative, they may allocate more land and resources to these crops, reducing the availability of land for non-supported crops. This can lead to price distortions and supply shortages in non-MSP crops, impacting the profitability and viability of those sectors. Additionally, fluctuations in MSP-supported crop prices can influence input costs for other agricultural activities, such as animal husbandry and horticulture, further affecting overall agricultural dynamics.

Welfare Implications of Minimum Support Price

Distributional Effects on Producers and Consumers

MSP mechanism plays a crucial role in redistributing income and alleviating poverty, impacting both producers (farmers) and consumers. Understanding these distributional effects is essential for evaluating the overall welfare implications of MSP policies.

a. **Income Redistribution and Poverty Alleviation:** MSP policies typically aim to ensure that farmers receive a fair price for their produce, thereby enhancing their income levels. By setting a floor price for agricultural commodities, MSP can stabilize farm incomes, particularly for smallholder farmers who are vulnerable to price fluctuations in the market. This income stabilization effect is significant in reducing poverty among rural farming communities, as agriculture remains a primary source of livelihood for a large portion of the population in many developing countries.

Furthermore, MSP can contribute to reducing income inequality by providing a safety net for small and marginal farmers who may lack bargaining power in the market. By guaranteeing a minimum price for their crops, MSP programs can help bridge the income gap between large commercial farmers and small-scale producers, thus promoting greater equity in agricultural income distribution.

b. **Consumer Surplus and Deadweight Loss:** While MSP policies benefit producers, they can also have adverse effects on consumers, particularly if the MSP is set above the market-clearing price. This scenario can lead to a reduction in consumer surplus, as consumers end up paying higher prices for agricultural products. Additionally, when MSP leads to overproduction due to artificially inflated prices, it can result in deadweight loss, representing a loss of economic efficiency.

The extent of these adverse effects depends on various factors, including the elasticity of demand for agricultural products, the level of government intervention in setting MSP and the efficiency of procurement and distribution mechanisms. Policymakers need to carefully balance the interests of producers and consumers to minimize deadweight loss while ensuring that farmers receive a fair income.

Equity and Efficiency Trade-Offs in MSP Implementation

a. **Targeting Vulnerable Farmer Groups:** One of the major challenges in MSP implementation is ensuring that the benefits reach the intended beneficiaries, particularly small and marginal farmers who are most vulnerable to market risks. In many cases, large farmers or agribusinesses may capture a significant portion of MSP benefits, leaving smallholders marginalized (Yogi *et al.*, 2018).

   To address this equity concern, policymakers need to design MSP programs with targeted measures to prioritize the inclusion of vulnerable farmer groups. This may involve implementing quotas or reservation policies to ensure that a certain percentage of MSP procurement is reserved for small-scale farmers. Additionally, investments in rural infrastructure, extension services and market linkages can empower smallholders to effectively participate in MSP schemes.

b. **Cost-Benefit Analysis of MSP Programs:** Assessing the overall effectiveness of MSP programs requires a comprehensive cost-benefit analysis that considers both the direct costs of procurement and the broader socioeconomic impacts. While MSP can provide short-term benefits in terms of income support and poverty alleviation, it is essential to evaluate the long-term sustainability and efficiency of these interventions.

Cost-benefit analysis should account for factors such as the opportunity cost of resources allocated to MSP procurement, the implications for fiscal sustainability and the potential distortions created in agricultural markets. Moreover, policymakers need to consider alternative policy instruments, such as income support schemes or investment in agricultural research and development, which may offer more cost-effective approaches to achieving similar welfare objectives (Srinivasa *et al.*, 2023).

The welfare implications of MSP policies are multifaceted, involving complex trade-offs between equity and efficiency. By carefully examining the distributional effects on producers and consumers, addressing equity concerns in MSP implementation, and conducting rigorous cost-benefit analysis, policymakers can design more effective and sustainable agricultural support mechanisms that promote inclusive growth and poverty reduction.

Policy Recommendations and Reform Strategies

Improving MSP Effectiveness and Targeting

a. Mechanisms for Ensuring Price Floors Reach Farmers:

- **Direct Procurement:** Establish a more efficient and transparent system for direct procurement from farmers to ensure that MSP benefits reach them directly. This can involve leveraging technology such as mobile apps or online platforms to streamline the procurement process.
- **Strengthening Farmer Producer Organizations (FPOs):** Empower FPOs to negotiate with procurement agencies on behalf of farmers, ensuring better representation and bargaining power. Provide support to FPOs through capacity building, training, and financial assistance.
- **Decentralized Procurement Centres:** Establish decentralized procurement centres closer to agricultural regions to reduce transportation costs and enhance accessibility for farmers, particularly in remote areas.

b. Enhancing Price Discovery Mechanisms

- **Market Intelligence Systems:** Invest in robust market intelligence systems to track price trends and demand-supply dynamics in real-time. This will enable policymakers to make informed decisions regarding MSP adjustments.
- **Strengthening Agricultural Marketing Infrastructure:** Improve infrastructure such as storage facilities, cold chains and transportation networks to reduce post-harvest losses and facilitate better price realization for farmers.

- **Promoting Contract Farming:** Encourage contract farming arrangements between farmers and agribusinesses to provide price predictability and reduce market risks. Establish regulatory frameworks to ensure fair contracts and protect farmers' interests.

Gradual Transition towards Market-Based Agricultural Policies

a. Subsidy Rationalization and Phasing Out MSP

- **Targeted Subsidy Programs:** Shift from blanket subsidies towards targeted subsidy programs that benefit small and marginalized farmers the most. This could involve income-based subsidies or subsidies linked to specific inputs such as seeds, fertilizers and irrigation.
- **Pilot Programs and Impact Assessments:** Conduct pilot programs to test the effectiveness of reducing MSP and gradually phase out the program based on empirical evidence and impact assessments. Monitor the socio-economic implications on farmers' income and welfare during the transition period.
- **Investment in Agricultural Research and Extension:** Redirect resources towards agricultural research and extension services to improve productivity and competitiveness in the absence of MSP. Focus on developing drought-resistant crops, efficient farming techniques and sustainable agricultural practices.

b. Strengthening Risk Management and Income Support Programs

- **Crop Insurance Schemes:** Enhance crop insurance schemes to provide comprehensive coverage against yield losses, price fluctuations and weather-related risks. Make insurance products more affordable and accessible to smallholder farmers by subsidizing premiums and simplifying claim procedures.
- **Income Support Schemes:** Introduce income support schemes such as direct cash transfers or income guarantees to provide a safety net for farmers during periods of low prices or production losses. Ensure that income support programs are well-targeted and complement existing risk management measures.
- **Diversification and Value Addition:** Encourage diversification into high-value crops and non-farm activities to mitigate income volatility and enhance resilience to market fluctuations. Support value addition initiatives through processing facilities and market linkages to capture higher margins along the value chain.

Conclusion

MSP policy of India aims to ensure farmers' income and stabilize agricultural markets. While well-intentioned, the program faces critiques. Setting MSPs involves a complex interplay of factors like production costs, global prices, and political considerations. MSP can incentivize certain crops, potentially leading to monoculture and inefficient resource use. Additionally, effectively reaching all farmers with MSP benefits remains a challenge. The debate centres on achieving a balance between efficiency and equity. Reforms like improved MSP targeting, better price discovery mechanisms, and a gradual shift towards market-oriented policies are crucial. Strengthening alternative income support programs and risk management strategies can provide a safety net for farmers while promoting a more dynamic agricultural sector.

References

Aditya, K. S., Subash, S. P., Praveen, K. V., Nithyashree, M. L., Bhuvana, N., & Sharma, A. (2017). Awareness about minimum support price and its impact on diversification decision of farmers in India. Asia & the Pacific Policy Studies, 4(3), 514-526.

Bhattarai, B. K., & GC, A. (2020). Government intervention strategy in agriculture price policy: a case of minimum support price in Nepal.

Chintapalli, P., & Tang, C. S. (2021). The value and cost of crop minimum support price: Farmer and consumer welfare and implementation cost. Management Science, 67(11), 6839-6861.

Chintapalli, P., & Tang, C. S. (2022). Crop minimum support price versus cost subsidy: Farmer and consumer welfare. Production and Operations Management, 31(4), 1753-1769.

Chintapalli, P., & Tang, C. S. (2022). The implications of crop minimum support price in the presence of myopic and strategic farmers. European Journal of Operational Research, 300(1), 336-349.

Geetha, R. S., & Mahesh, V. (2019). Minimum support prices (MSP) and its influence on cotton farming in India. Asian Journal of Agricultural Extension, Economics & Sociology, 30(4), 1-8.

Janaiah, A., & Shireesha, A. A. K. (2020). Growth Performance and its Sources Vis-à-Vis Minimum Support Price of Cotton in Telangana State. Int. J. Curr. Microbiol. App. Sci, 9(12), 599-606.

Kumar, K., & Mazhar, S. H. (2021). An Analytical Study of Relationship between Socio-Economic Profile and Impact of Minimum Support Price Scheme on Small Farmers of Begusarai District of Bihar.

Kumar, M., Sharma, M., & Kumar, K. (2021). Minimum support price for agricultural commodities in India: A review. Pharma Innov. J, 10, 12-16.

Mahto, R., & Patil, C. (2023). Analyzing the Impact of Minimum Support Price Policy on Area, Production and Productivity of Finger Millet (Ragi) in India: A Comprehensive Analysis of Trends, CAGR and Associations. Research Journal of Agricultural Sciences, 14(3), 668-671.

Mahto, R., & Patil, C. (2023). Minimum Support Price and Its Effect on Area, Production and Productivity of Gram in India. Research Journal of Agricultural Sciences, 14(3), 683-686.

Prabha, S. A., Murugananthi, D., & Palanichamy, N. V. (2023). A comprehensive analysis of minimum support price on area, production and yield of pearl millet (Bajra) in India. Indian Journal of Agricultural Marketing, 37(3spl), 91-91.

Srinivasa, A. K., Praveen, K. V., Padmaja, S. S., Nithyashree, M. L., & Jha, G. K. (2023). Does a farmer's knowledge of minimum support price (MSP) affect the farm-gate price? Evidence from India. Journal of Economics and Development, 25(4), 302-316.

Visnu, S.D., & Babu, S. (2023). Advanced agronomics model with species classification, minimum support price prediction, and profit suggestion using enhanced deep learning strategy. Knowledge and Information Systems, 65(3), 1243-1285.

Yogi, R. K., Singh, A. K., Kumar, N., & Sharma, K. K. (2018). Assessing Minimum Support Price for Non-Wood Forest Products (NWFPs): A Priority based Policy Intervention in India.

2

Financial Markets The Lifeline of Economies

Harshit Mishra*, Divyanshi Mishra and Manaswini, N.

Department of Agricultural Economics, College of Agriculture, Acharya Narendra Deva University of Agriculture and Technology, Kumarganj, Ayodhya (U.P.)

Abstract

Agriculture, feeding billions, underpins economies. Yet, its success hinges on a healthy financial system. Financial markets, the lifeblood of economies, perform several critical functions. Firstly, they channel savings – like those from profitable farms – towards investments in seeds, equipment and infrastructure. This facilitates capital allocation, matching risk tolerance with opportunities. For example, farmers seeking capital for expansion can find it through these markets. Additionally, financial markets mobilize capital for growth. Businesses can raise funds to expand production or develop innovative farming techniques. Additionally, governments can finance vital projects like irrigation systems through bond sales. Financial markets further enhance liquidity and price discovery. Farmers can easily sell their produce and access working capital. Prices are determined by supply and demand, reflecting true market value. There are different types of financial markets. Money markets deal with short-term debt instruments, vital for businesses and banks managing cash flow. Capital markets, on the other hand, provide long-term equity and debt financing for businesses, allowing farms to invest in long-term growth. Finally, derivatives markets offer risk management tools like futures contracts, which can help farmers hedge against price fluctuations. Financial institutions play a crucial role. Banks accept deposits from individuals (including those saving surplus farm income) and provide loans to farmers for operational needs. Investment banks help farms raise capital by underwriting stock or bond offerings. Insurance companies and pension funds pool risks and manage long-term savings, contributing to overall financial stability. Regulation is essential to prevent fraud, ensure transparency and protect investors. Effective risk management helps mitigate systemic risks that can lead to financial crises. By ensuring a healthy financial system, financial markets act as the lifeline that nourishes not just agriculture, but the entire economy.

Keywords: *Capital Allocation, Growth, Investment, Liquidity, Risk Management*

Introduction

Since the dawn of agriculture, humans have bartered and traded goods and services. Financial markets represent a sophisticated evolution of this basic need to exchange value. Today, they act as the invisible backbone of economies, playing a critical role in channelling resources, facilitating growth, and enabling price discovery. Financial markets fulfil three key functions that keep economies humming. Firstly, they facilitate capital allocation. Imagine a farmer with surplus earnings (savings) from a bountiful harvest (Schar, 2021). In the absence of financial markets, these savings may sit idle. But financial markets connect this farmer with businesses seeking investment capital to expand operations or develop new technologies. According to a 2023 World Bank report, global gross savings reached a staggering $36 trillion, highlighting the immense pool of resources financial markets can tap. This allocation function goes a step further by matching risk tolerance with investment opportunities. A conservative investor seeking stability might favour government bonds, while a risk-tolerant entrepreneur may invest in a promising startup. Financial markets offer instruments to cater to diverse risk appetites, ensuring a healthy balance between stability and growth (Umar *et al.*, 2022).

Financial markets don't just connect savers and investors; they also mobilize capital for economic growth. Businesses seeking to expand can raise funds through stock offerings, allowing them to build new factories, hire additional staff and develop innovative products. A 2022 study by the International Finance Corporation found that small and medium-sized businesses in emerging markets face a financing gap of over $5 trillion. Financial markets play a vital role in bridging this gap, fostering business expansion, and driving long-term economic prosperity. Furthermore, financial markets enable governments to finance critical infrastructure projects like roads, bridges, and public transportation. By issuing bonds, governments can raise vast sums of capital to invest in projects that benefit society (Pagano, 1993).

Financial markets also enhance liquidity and price discovery. Liquidity refers to the ease with which an asset can be bought or sold. Financial markets provide a platform for investors to easily buy and sell financial instruments, ensuring a healthy flow of capital. This liquidity is crucial for businesses seeking to raise funds quickly or investors who need to adjust their portfolios. Price discovery is another vital function (Bailey, 2005). Through the dynamic interplay of supply and demand in financial markets, the fair market value of an asset is established. This price reflects the collective wisdom of investors and helps businesses make informed investment decisions.

The financial market ecosystem encompasses a variety of specialized markets, each serving a distinct purpose. Money markets, for instance, deal with short-term debt instruments like treasury bills and commercial paper. These markets allow businesses and banks to manage their short-term liquidity needs. Capital markets, on the other hand, focus on long-term investments. Businesses raise capital through stock offerings (equity financing) or bond issuance (debt financing) in capital markets. These markets provide companies with the resources needed for long-term growth and innovation. A third type, the derivatives market, offers risk management tools like options and futures contracts. These instruments allow investors to hedge against price fluctuations, mitigating potential losses in volatile markets.

Financial institutions play a crucial role in the smooth functioning of financial markets. Banks and credit unions act as intermediaries, accepting deposits from individuals and providing loans to businesses and consumers. They also facilitate payments and money transfers, greasing the wheels of commerce. Investment banks and brokerage firms underwrite securities, connect investors with investment opportunities and offer valuable financial advice. Insurance companies and pension funds pool risks and manage long-term savings, contributing to the overall stability of financial markets. Financial markets thrive on trust and transparency. To ensure this, a robust regulatory framework is essential. Regulatory bodies implement rules to prevent fraud, market manipulation and insider trading. These regulations protect investors and promote fair market practices.

Financial markets are inherently risky. Systemic risks, such as a global financial crisis, can trigger widespread economic instability. To mitigate these risks, financial institutions and regulators employ various strategies. Diversification, for example, encourages spreading investments across different asset classes to minimize losses from any single asset class experiencing a downturn. Additionally, capital adequacy requirements ensure that financial institutions maintain sufficient reserves to weather financial storms (Ang and Timmermann, 2012). Financial markets are the lifeblood of modern economies. They efficiently allocate capital, mobilize resources for growth and facilitate price discovery. The diverse landscape of financial markets, supported by a network of institutions and a robust regulatory framework, ensures the smooth flow of funds that keeps economies humming. By constantly innovating and adapting to evolving needs, financial markets will continue to play a vital role in shaping a more prosperous and secure future (Mishkin and Eakins, 2006).

Functions of Financial Markets

Financial markets play a crucial role in the economy by facilitating various functions that ensure efficient allocation of capital, mobilization of funds for growth and enhancing liquidity and price discovery. In this section, we will discuss these functions in detail.

Facilitating Capital Allocation

a. **Channelling Savings to Investment:** One of the primary functions of financial markets is to channel savings from households, businesses, and governments into productive investment opportunities. Individuals and entities with surplus funds, such as savings, pension funds, or insurance companies, seek avenues to invest their money to earn returns. On the other hand, businesses and governments require capital to fund their operations, expansions, or projects. Financial markets act as intermediaries, connecting savers with borrowers by providing a platform for the issuance and trading of various financial instruments such as stocks, bonds and derivatives. This process efficiently allocates capital to projects and ventures that offer the highest returns relative to their risk profile, thereby promoting economic growth and development.

b. **Matching Risk Tolerance with Investment Opportunities:** Financial markets offer a wide array of investment options with varying risk-return profiles. Investors have different risk preferences and investment objectives based on factors such as age, income, and financial goals. Financial markets play a critical role in matching the risk tolerance of investors with suitable investment opportunities. For instance, risk-averse investors may prefer low-risk assets such as government bonds or blue-chip stocks, while risk-seeking investors may opt for higher-risk investments like equities of emerging companies or speculative derivatives. By providing a diverse range of investment instruments, financial markets ensure that investors can allocate their capital in alignment with their risk preferences, thereby optimizing their investment portfolios.

Mobilizing Capital for Growth

a. **Supporting Business Expansion and Innovation:** Financial markets play a vital role in mobilizing capital for businesses, enabling them to finance expansion plans, research and development initiatives and innovation projects. Through the issuance of equity (stocks) and debt (bonds), companies can raise funds from investors to invest in new technologies, infrastructure, and human capital. Access to capital markets allows businesses to grow and remain competitive in dynamic market environments. Moreover, the ability to raise funds through financial markets reduces reliance on traditional bank loans, diversifying funding sources and spreading risks across a broader investor base.

b. **Financing Government Projects and Infrastructure:** Governments also rely on financial markets to finance public projects, infrastructure development, and social welfare programs. Sovereign bonds issued by governments are traded in financial markets, allowing them to raise funds from domestic and international investors. These funds are then utilized for critical infrastructure projects such as roads, bridges, schools, and healthcare facilities. By tapping into financial markets, governments can address funding gaps, stimulate economic growth, and enhance the overall quality of life for citizens. Additionally, financial markets play a role in fiscal management by providing governments with tools such as treasury bonds and bills to manage liquidity and debt levels effectively (Bond *et al.*, 2012).

Enhancing Liquidity and Price Discovery

a. **Enabling Easy Buying and Selling of Financial Assets:** Financial markets enhance liquidity by providing a platform for easy buying and selling of financial assets. Liquidity refers to the ease with which an asset can be converted into cash without significantly affecting its price. Liquid markets allow investors to enter and exit positions quickly, enabling efficient capital allocation and risk management. In liquid markets, there is a constant flow of buy and sell orders, which ensures that asset prices reflect the true underlying value based on market supply and demand dynamics. This liquidity not only benefits investors but also fosters market efficiency and stability.

b. **Determining Fair Market Value Through Supply and Demand:** Financial markets facilitate price discovery by bringing together buyers and sellers to determine the fair market value of assets. The interplay of supply and demand forces in financial markets results in price movements that reflect the collective wisdom and expectations of market participants. Through continuous trading activities, market prices adjust to new information, changing economic conditions and investor sentiment. Price discovery is essential for ensuring that assets are valued, which fosters confidence and trust in the financial system. Moreover, accurate price signals help investors make informed decisions regarding buying, selling, or holding assets, thereby contributing to market efficiency and resource allocation.

Financial markets serve as the lifeline of economies by performing essential functions such as facilitating capital allocation, mobilizing funds for growth, and enhancing liquidity and price discovery. These functions are crucial for promoting economic development, fostering innovation, and ensuring the efficient allocation of resources in a dynamic and interconnected global economy (Pilbeam, 2018).

Different Types of Financial Markets

Financial markets are indispensible components of any economy, serving as conduits for the allocation of capital and the management of risk. They provide avenues for individuals, businesses, and governments to raise funds, invest capital and hedge against uncertainties. To understand the various types of financial markets (as shown in Table 1) is essential for comprehending how these mechanisms facilitate economic growth and stability.

Money Markets

Money markets are integral to the efficient functioning of financial systems, primarily dealing with short-term debt instruments and providing liquidity management solutions for participants. Two key instruments commonly traded in money markets are Treasury Bills (T-bills) and Commercial Paper.

a. Short-Term Debt Instruments

- **Treasury Bills (T-bills):** These are short-term debt securities issued by governments, typically with maturities ranging from a few days to one year. They are considered low-risk investments and are highly liquid, making them attractive options for investors seeking safe-haven assets.
- **Commercial Paper:** This is a short-term debt instrument issued by corporations to raise funds for operational expenses, such as payroll and inventory management. Commercial paper typically matures within 270 days and offers higher yields compared to T-bills, reflecting the credit risk associated with the issuing corporation.

b. Function: Balancing Liquidity Needs for Businesses and Banks

- Money markets play a vital role in balancing the liquidity needs of businesses, banks and other financial institutions. By providing a platform for the trading of short-term debt instruments, money markets ensure that entities can efficiently manage their cash flows and meet their immediate funding requirements.
- Additionally, money markets serve as avenues for central banks to implement monetary policy by influencing short-term interest rates and regulating the money supply.

Capital Markets

Capital markets facilitate long-term investments and play a fundamental role in channelling capital from investors to businesses and governments. Key instruments traded in capital markets include stocks (equities) and bonds (fixed-income securities).

a. Long-Term Investments

- **Stocks (Equities):** Stocks represent ownership stakes in publicly traded companies, entitling shareholders to a portion of the company's profits and voting rights in corporate decisions. Investing in stocks offers the potential for capital appreciation through increases in share prices and dividend payments.
- **Bonds (Fixed-Income Securities):** Bonds are debt instruments issued by governments, corporations, or municipalities to raise capital. Bondholders receive periodic interest payments (coupon payments) and the return of principal upon maturity. Bonds are classified based on their issuer (government bonds, corporate bonds, municipal bonds) and maturity (short-term, medium-term, long-term).

b. Function: Providing Equity and Debt Capital for Businesses

- Capital markets serve as primary platforms for businesses to raise equity and debt capital to finance their operations, expansion projects and investments in innovation.
- Equity financing, facilitated through the issuance of stocks, enables businesses to raise funds without incurring debt obligations, while debt financing, facilitated through the issuance of bonds, allows businesses to access capital by borrowing funds from investors in exchange for periodic interest payments and repayment of principal.
- By enabling efficient allocation of capital, capital markets contribute to economic growth, job creation and innovation, fostering entrepreneurship and corporate development.

Derivatives Markets

Derivatives markets provide instruments for managing and mitigating risks associated with price fluctuations in underlying assets, serving as essential tools for risk management and speculation.

a. Risk Management Tools

- **Options:** Options provide the buyer with the right, but not the obligation, to buy (call option) or sell (put option) an underlying asset at a predetermined price (strike price) within a specified period. Options are used for hedging against adverse price movements and for speculation on future price movements.
- **Futures Contracts:** Futures contracts are agreements to buy or sell a specified asset at a predetermined price on a future date. Futures contracts are standardized and traded on organized exchanges, facilitating price

discovery and liquidity. They are commonly used for hedging against price risk and for speculative purposes by investors seeking to profit from anticipated price movements.

b. Function: Hedging Against Price Fluctuations

- Derivatives markets play a critical role in enabling market participants to hedge against price fluctuations in underlying assets, such as commodities, currencies, stocks and interest rates.
- Hedging strategies using options and futures contracts help businesses and investors mitigate risks arising from adverse price movements, thereby safeguarding profits and preserving capital.
- Additionally, derivatives markets provide opportunities for speculation and arbitrage, enhancing market efficiency and liquidity while contributing to price discovery mechanisms.

Table 1: Differences between Money, Capital and Derivatives Markets

Aspect	**Money Market**	**Capital Market**	**Derivatives Market**
Purpose	Short-term borrowing and lending	Long-term investment and funding	Hedging and speculation
Instruments	Treasury bills, commercial paper	Stocks, bonds, mortgages	Options, futures, swaps
Maturity	Usually up to 1 year	Over 1 year	Contracts vary (short to long term)
Risk Level	Generally lower risk	Moderate to high risk	High risk, depending on instrument
Regulation	Typically, highly regulated	Moderately regulated	Varies by jurisdiction
Liquidity	High liquidity	Moderate liquidity	Varies by instrument and market
Participants	Banks, financial institutions, institutional investors	Corporations, governments, institutional investors	Financial institutions, investors, corporations
Example Institutions	Federal Reserve, commercial banks	Stock exchanges, investment banks	Chicago Mercantile Exchange

Financial markets encompass a diverse array of instruments and functions, ranging from short-term liquidity management in money markets to long-term capital allocation in capital markets and risk management in derivatives markets. These markets form the backbone of modern economies, facilitating efficient resource allocation, risk transfer and economic growth (Stiglitz, 1993).

The Role of Financial Institutions

Financial institutions play a crucial role in the functioning of financial markets and are often considered the backbone of economies. They provide various services that facilitate the flow of funds between savers and borrowers, investors and issuers and individuals and businesses. This section delves into the specific functions and contributions of different types of financial institutions.

Banks and Credit Unions

a. **Accepting Deposits and Providing Loans:** Banks and credit unions are primary depository institutions that accept deposits from individuals, businesses, and other entities. These deposits serve as a stable source of funds for banks, which they utilize to extend loans to borrowers. By accepting deposits, banks play a critical role in providing liquidity to depositors while simultaneously allocating capital to borrowers for various purposes such as personal loans, mortgages and business financing. This function is fundamental to economic growth as it ensures the efficient allocation of capital to productive uses, thereby fostering investment, consumption and overall economic activity.

b. **Facilitating Payments and Money Transfers:** Another essential role of banks and credit unions is facilitating payments and money transfers within and across borders. Through various channels such as checks, electronic fund transfers (EFTs), wire transfers and digital payment systems, financial institutions enable the seamless exchange of funds between parties. This function enhances the efficiency of transactions, reduces transaction costs and promotes economic transactions by providing individuals and businesses with convenient and reliable means of transferring money (Pandey *et al.,* 2023).

Investment Banks and Brokerage Firms

a. **Underwriting Securities and Facilitating Stock Market Transactions:** Investment banks play a vital role in the issuance of securities by corporations and governments. They assist in underwriting new securities offerings, including initial public offerings (IPOs), debt securities and equity offerings. By underwriting these securities, investment banks assume the risk of purchasing the securities from the issuer and reselling them to investors, thereby facilitating the capital-raising process for issuers. Additionally, brokerage firms enable investors to buy and sell securities in financial markets by providing brokerage services. These firms execute trades on behalf of clients in stock exchanges and other trading platforms, facilitating liquidity and price discovery in financial markets.

b. **Providing Investment Advice and Asset Management Services:** Investment banks and brokerage firms also offer investment advice and asset management services to individuals, institutions, and corporations. Through research analysis, financial modelling and market insights, these institutions provide clients with recommendations and strategies for investing in various asset classes such as stocks, bonds, mutual funds, and alternative investments. Additionally, asset management services involve the professional management of investment portfolios on behalf of clients, aiming to achieve their financial goals while managing risk and maximizing returns.

Insurance Companies and Pension Funds

a. **Risk Pooling and Long-Term Savings Management:** Insurance companies and pension funds play critical roles in managing risks and facilitating long-term savings and investments. Insurance companies offer various types of insurance products, including life insurance, health insurance, property and casualty insurance and annuities. These products enable individuals and businesses to pool risks and protect against unforeseen events such as accidents, illnesses, natural disasters, and loss of income. Similarly, pension funds manage retirement savings on behalf of individuals and employees, providing a vehicle for long-term wealth accumulation and retirement income.

b. **Contributing to Financial Market Stability:** Furthermore, insurance companies and pension funds contribute to financial market stability by diversifying investment portfolios and providing stability to capital markets. Through their long-term investment horizon and risk management practices, these institutional investors stabilize financial markets by absorbing shocks and maintaining liquidity during periods of market volatility. Additionally, their substantial assets under management (AUM) provide a stable source of funding for capital markets, promoting liquidity and efficiency in the allocation of capital (Albulescu, 2021).

Financial institutions perform various functions that are essential for the efficient functioning of financial markets and the overall economy. From facilitating savings and investments to providing liquidity, risk management and financial intermediation services, these institutions play a pivotal role in channelling funds between surplus and deficit units, supporting economic growth and maintaining financial stability.

Regulation and Risk Management in Financial Markets

Financial markets play a pivotal role in the economy by facilitating the allocation of capital, enabling investment and growth. However, to ensure the stability and integrity of these markets, regulation and risk management are essential components. This section delves into the importance of regulation and the strategies employed for managing financial risks.

Importance of Regulation

Regulation serves as a safeguard against various risks and malpractices that could jeopardize the functioning of financial markets.

a. **Preventing Fraud and Market Manipulation:** One of the primary objectives of financial regulation is to prevent fraud and market manipulation. Fraudulent activities, such as insider trading or Ponzi schemes, can distort market prices and erode investor confidence. Regulations such as the Securities Exchange Act of 1934 in the United States or the Markets in Financial Instruments Directive (MiFID) in Europe aim to combat such practices by imposing stringent reporting requirements, conducting regular audits and enforcing severe penalties for violations (Zhang *et al.*, 2020).

b. **Ensuring Market Transparency and Investor Protection:** Regulations also aim to ensure market transparency and protect the interests of investors. Transparency is crucial for maintaining trust in financial markets, as it allows investors to make informed decisions based on accurate information. Regulations such as the requirement for companies to disclose financial information regularly or the implementation of fair-trading practices contribute to enhancing market transparency. Moreover, investor protection measures, such as the establishment of regulatory bodies like the Securities and Exchange Commission (SEC) in the U.S. or the Financial Conduct Authority (FCA) in the UK, are vital for safeguarding investors' rights and interests.

Managing Financial Risks

Financial markets are inherently exposed to various risks, ranging from market volatility to systemic crises. Effective risk management is crucial for mitigating these risks and maintaining stability in the financial system.

a. **Systemic Risk and Financial Crises:** Systemic risk refers to the risk of widespread disruption or collapse of the financial system, often triggered by interconnectedness among financial institutions or market participants. Financial crises, such as the 2008 global financial crisis, underscore the significance of systemic risk. Regulations such as Basel III, introduced in response to the 2008 crisis, aim to enhance the resilience of financial institutions and mitigate systemic risk by imposing stricter capital adequacy requirements, liquidity standards and stress testing protocols (Sansa, 2020).

b. **Strategies for Mitigating Risk:** Diversification and capital adequacy are key strategies for mitigating financial risks.

- **Diversification:** Diversifying investments across different asset classes, sectors and geographical regions can help investors reduce the impact of market volatility and specific risks associated with individual assets. By spreading risk, diversification aims to achieve a balance between risk and return.
- **Capital Adequacy:** Ensuring that financial institutions maintain adequate capital reserves is essential for absorbing potential losses and safeguarding against insolvency. Regulatory frameworks such as Basel Accords prescribe minimum capital requirements based on the risk profile of assets held by financial institutions. By enhancing capital adequacy, regulators aim to strengthen the resilience of financial institutions and mitigate the likelihood of systemic crises.

Regulation and risk management are indispensable components of financial markets, essential for maintaining stability, integrity, and investor confidence. Through robust regulatory frameworks and effective risk management strategies, financial markets can fulfil their role as the lifeline of economies, facilitating sustainable growth and development.

Conclusion

Financial markets play a critical role in a healthy economy. By efficiently allocating capital (estimated at over $360 trillion globally in 2023), they connect those with surplus funds (savers) to those seeking investment (businesses and governments). This fuels business expansion, innovation, and infrastructure development, fostering economic growth. A variety of markets exist, each serving a specific purpose. Money markets, with instruments like treasury bills (maturing in under a year), address short-term liquidity needs. Capital markets, including stock exchanges, provide long-term financing through stocks and bonds. Derivative markets, like options contracts, allow for risk management against unforeseen price fluctuations. Financial institutions like banks, brokerage firms, and insurance companies act as facilitators, enabling transactions, offering investment advice, and managing long-term savings. These entities contribute to market stability, but regulations are crucial to prevent fraud and ensure investor protection. Effective risk management strategies, including diversification and capital adequacy requirements, further safeguard the system from crises. Well-functioning financial markets act as the lifeblood of an economy, channelling resources for growth and innovation while mitigating risks.

References

Albulescu, C.T. (2021). COVID-19 and the United States financial markets' volatility. Finance research letters, 38, 101699.

Ang, A., & Timmermann, A. (2012). Regime changes and financial markets. Annu. Rev. Financ. Econ., 4(1), 313-337.

Bailey, R. E. (2005). The economics of financial markets. Cambridge University Press.

Bond, P., Edmans, A., & Goldstein, I. (2012). The real effects of financial markets. Annu. Rev. Financ. Econ., 4(1), 339-360.

Mishkin, F. S., & Eakins, S. G. (2006). Financial markets and institutions. Pearson Education India.

Pagano, M. (1993). Financial markets and growth: An overview. European economic review, 37(2-3), 613-622.

Pandey, D. K., Lucey, B. M., & Kumar, S. (2023). Border disputes, conflicts, war, and financial markets research: a systematic review. Research in International Business and Finance, 101972.

Pilbeam, K. (2018). Finance and financial markets. Bloomsbury Publishing.

Sansa, N. A. (2020). The Impact of the COVID-19 on the Financial Markets: Evidence from China and USA. Electronic Research Journal of Social Sciences and Humanities, 2.

Schär, F. (2021). Decentralized finance: On blockchain-and smart contract-based financial markets. FRB of St. Louis Review.

Stiglitz, J. E. (1993). The role of the state in financial markets. The world bank economic review, 7(suppl_1), 19-52.

Umar, Z., Polat, O., Choi, S. Y., & Teplova, T. (2022). The impact of the Russia-Ukraine conflict on the connectedness of financial markets. Finance Research Letters, 48, 102976.

Zhang, D., Hu, M., & Ji, Q. (2020). Financial markets under the global pandemic of COVID-19. Finance research letters, 36, 101528.

3

Dynamics of Agricultural Economics and Minimum Support Prices

***Sandeep Gautam*[1], *Shiv Kumar Rana*[2], *Abhishek Raj Ranjan*[3]**

[1]*Department of Agricultural Economics, Acharya Narendra Deva University of Agriculture & Technology, Ayodhya, Uttar Pradesh*

[2]*Department of Agricultural Statistics, Acharya Narendra Deva University of Agriculture & Technology, Ayodhya, Uttar Pradesh*

[3]*Department of Agronomy, Banda University of Agriculture & Technology Banda, Uttar Pradesh*

Abstract

A variety of factors, such as price dynamics and the effects of government interventions such as Minimum Support Prices (MSPs) on crop productivity and farmer welfare, are included in the field of agricultural economics dynamics and have an impact on how the agricultural sector functions. Several factors, including price mechanisms, the significance of inventories, and how price volatility affects farmers' earnings, have an impact on the dynamics of agricultural markets. MSPs and other government initiatives are intended to shield farmers from market swings and guarantee sufficient agricultural output. Farmers' incomes can be impacted by MSPs; if MSPs are set too low, there may be a chance for lower earnings. On the other hand, well-selected MSPs can enhance general welfare and benefit all farmers. Offering MSPs for commodities that complement one another can also increase farmers' surplus. The impact of Minimum Support Prices (MSP) on crop production, farmer welfare, and price dynamics is the main topic of the abstract for the dynamics of agricultural economics and MSPs. Furthermore, the abstract emphasizes the function of government price support programs in agriculture economics and the significance of MSP in affecting price dynamics and volatility.

Keywords: *Dynamics, Government interventions, Minimum Support Prices, Price volatility.*

Introduction

The most important function in the socioeconomic domain of India is played by agriculture, which is the foundation of the nation's economy. India's agriculture industry is vast, varied, and involves a lot of different players. With the use of Green Revolution technologies, it has become one of the most amazing success stories of the post-independence era. The Green Revolution enhanced rural welfare and allowed for food self-sufficiency, both of which boosted the Indian economy. In the framework of the Green Revolution, the National Agricultural Research System (NARS) played a crucial role. India boasts one of the world's biggest and most intricate agricultural research programs in terms of structure. The Imperial (now Indian) Council of Agricultural Research (ICAR) was established in 1929 on the advice of a Royal Commission on Agriculture, marking the culmination of a process that began in the 19th century and led to the creation of the current Indian agricultural research system [1].

The functioning of the agricultural sector, market dynamics, and policy consequences are all influenced by a complex web of interrelated components that make up agricultural economics dynamics. These dynamics shape the production, supply, demand, and competitiveness of agricultural products and involve the interactions between farmers, markets, technology, and government regulations [2],[5].

Key aspects of the Dynamics of Agricultural Economics Include

Market Forces: Market factors including supply and demand dynamics, price swings, and consumer preferences have an impact on agricultural economics. The interplay among these variables establishes the farming methods' profitability and sustainability [5].

Policy Impact: A vital role is played by government programs such as the Minimum Support Price (MSP), which give farmers a stable source of income, impact production choices, and maintain market equilibrium [5].

Resource Allocation: Analysing resource allocation within the agricultural sector, including land use patterns, technology adoption, labour management, and investment decisions, is the focus of agricultural economics. Increasing agricultural production and profitability requires effective resource allocation [2].

Global Market Integration: Trade policies, international competition, and worldwide market trends are all having an increasing impact on the dynamics of agricultural economics. Local farming techniques are impacted by variables such as global price swings, import vulnerabilities, and export potential [5].

Sustainability Concerns: A significant area of interest in agricultural economic dynamics is environmental sustainability. To maintain ecological health and agricultural output over the long term, it is imperative to strike a balance between economic viability and environmental conservation [6].

Essentially, the dynamics of agricultural economics comprise a complex system of interconnectedness that includes market dynamics, governmental interventions, resource management, global effects, and sustainability considerations, all of which work together to define the agricultural sector's economic environment[17].

There are several ways in which the idea of the Minimum Support Price (MSP) and the dynamics of agricultural economics interact. Applying economic principles to agriculture and addressing issues that farmers, policymakers, and the agricultural industry confront are the main goals of the study of agricultural economics. To improve farm profitability, sustainability, and efficiency, analysis of variables such as resource allocation, production, market dynamics, and policy decisions is required. A measure that governments use to guarantee farmers get paid fairly for their produce, particularly for staple crops, is the Minimum Support Price (MSP). To shield farmers from market swings and provide financial security, MSP serves as a safety net by ensuring a minimum price for their products. Analysing how MSP affects farm income, market stability, and rural development is a critical task for agricultural economists. To help policymakers understand how well MSP supports farmers and the economy, they offer evidence-based insights [3].

A. What are the Potential Consequences of Government Policies on Agricultural Productivity?

The efficiency and results of agricultural activities are shaped by government policies, which may have a variety of effects on agricultural productivity. Based on the references given, the following are some significant possible outcomes:

1. **Impact on Production and Income:** Agriculture-related productivity, income levels, and other results can be impacted by government policies, including input, output, and technical subsidies. Numerous studies have examined the effects of financial supports, such as cash subsidies, credit, and tax benefits, on income and productivity, with differing conclusions drawn from the data[7].
2. **Influence on Land Allocation and Efficiency:** Policies can affect the distribution of land, productivity, and employment levels in agriculture. Research has demonstrated the impact of regulations on variables such as employment both on and off farm, area expansion, and crop

diversification, underscoring the wider implications of governmental involvement in agriculture[7].

3. **Structural Changes and Innovation:** Within the agricultural sector, government policies can stimulate innovation and bring about structural changes. The adoption of new technology, structural modifications, and innovation in agricultural practices can be influenced by policies including price and income support, investment assistance, input subsidies, and agri-environmental initiatives[8].
4. **Market Distortions and Incentives:** A few policy tools, including as supply restrictions, output-based pricing, and border protection, have the potential to skew markets and lessen producers' incentives to employ production variables more effectively. However, a broad-based income support program that is independent of the production of commodities can efficiently transfer revenue to producers, boosting their ability to make investments and innovate[8].

B. How Does MSP Affect Agricultural Economics

The Minimum Support Price (MSP) has a big effect on agricultural economics. Governments utilize MSP as a policy instrument to guarantee farmers get a fair price for their produce, giving them certainty in their income and shielding them from market fluctuations. On the other hand, MSP's effects on agriculture economics can be complicated.

1. **Impact on Farmers' Surplus:** MSP can have conflicting impacts on farmers because it can harm crop cultivators and reduce their surplus, particularly when myopic and strategically minded farmers are involved[9].
2. **Market Dynamics:** Farmers' awareness of these support prices determines how MSP affects farm-gate prices. The dynamics of the market may change if farmers are aware of MSPs and are able to negotiate better pricing.
3. **Regional Disparities:** The MSP policy has come under fire for disproportionately helping farmers in the states where procurement takes place, which has resulted in differences in benefit distribution between regions. This may influence the economic conditions in certain agricultural regions[10].
4. **Crop Production and Farmer Welfare:** In agricultural economics, one of the most important factors is how crop MSPs affect crop productivity and farmer welfare. MSP regulations may have an impact on the types of crops grown, output levels, and general farmer welfare[9].

5. **Risk Mitigation and Security:** MSP serves as a safeguard against market volatility, shielding farmers from sudden price declines and giving them a sense of stability in an unstable market[11].

C. How Does MSP Impact the Supply and Demand of Crops

Within the agricultural industry, the Minimum Support Price (MSP) affects crop supply and demand in a number of ways, including:[18,19]

Supply Side Effects

i. **Increased Production:** Because MSP guarantees farmers a minimum price for their products, it can encourage farmers to boost production. This guarantee motivates farmers to increase cultivation areas, use cutting-edge methods, and invest in high-quality inputs, all of which increase crop yields.

ii. **Buffer Stocks:** With MSP, the government can purchase crops at the guaranteed price, allowing it to accumulate buffer stockpiles. Consistent procurement can impact supply dynamics by guaranteeing a stable supply of necessary goods in times of scarcity or emergency.

Demand Side Effects

i. **Market Distortions:** MSP's detractors contend that by artificially setting a price, it might skew market dynamics and even cause inefficiencies. Demand patterns may be impacted by government procurement operations under MSP, which may lessen competition and deter private bidders[12].

ii. **Impact on Global Competitiveness:** Increased MSPs may diminish crops' ability to compete on the world market, which could lead to a decline in exports and trade disputes. This may influence the demand for specific crops abroad[13].

D. Benefits of Minimum Support Price (MSP) for farmers

The benefits of Minimum Support Price (MSP) for farmers include:

1. **Assured Income:** Farmers are shielded from market swings and given economic security by MSP, which guarantees a minimum price for their products.
2. **Market Stability:** By establishing a floor price below which market prices are incapable of falling, MSP contributes to price stabilization. Even in periods of excess output, farmers are guaranteed a fair price for their crop thanks to this stability.

3. **Government Procurement:** MSP plans sometimes entail the government buying crops at a predetermined price, which guarantees farmers' income and helps create buffer stocks for public distribution networks and food security.
4. **Financial Planning:** Farmers can forecast revenue using MSP as a benchmark, which helps with financial planning and influences borrowing decisions. It supports farmers in making well-informed decisions on investments and crop selection[14].
5. **Risk Mitigation:** MSP serves as a safeguard against market volatility, shielding farmers from abrupt price declines and giving them a sense of stability in an unstable market[15].
6. **Incentive for Production:** By guaranteeing farmers a minimum price for their crops, MSP encourages farmers to boost output. Farmers are encouraged by this guarantee to increase their crop areas, use contemporary farming methods, and invest in high-quality inputs[16].

Conclusion

To summarize, policies imposed by the government can have a substantial impact on agricultural productivity through their influence on various aspects of the agricultural sector, such as production levels, income, land distribution, efficiency, innovation, structural changes, and market incentives. While MSP acts as a policy tool to protect farmers' interests, agricultural economics explores the intricacies of farming and markets. Understanding the interplay between these factors is crucial to comprehending how market forces, MSP policies, and economic principles influence the sustainability and expansion of the agriculture industry. Through its effects on farmer income, market dynamics, regional disparities, crop choices, and general wellbeing within the agricultural sector, the Minimum Support Price (MSP) significantly shapes agricultural economics. To make well-informed decisions on agricultural policies and practices, stakeholders and policymakers must have a thorough understanding of the varied impact of MSP. Through incentives and buffer stock arrangements, the Minimum Support Price stimulates production, which in turn affects the supply side. MSP has the potential to distort markets and undermine global competitiveness, which could have an effect on the demand for crops both domestically and abroad. Overall, by giving farmers risk mitigation, market predictability, income stability, and production incentives, the Minimum Support Price (MSP) significantly improves their quality of life and that of the agricultural industry.

References

1. Borthakur, A. and Singh, P. (2012). Agricultural research in India: an exploratory study. International Journal of Social Science & Interdisciplinary Research, 1(9), 59-74.
2. Hebinck, P. G. M., and Ploeg, J. D. (1997). Dynamics of agricultural production. An analysis of micro-macro linkages. In Images and realities of rural life. Wageningen perspectives on rural transformations 202-226.
3. Rayes B. The intersection of agricultural economics: Navigating the dynamics of farming and markets. J Agric Sci Bot. 2023;7(4):188
4. Dohlman, E., Osborne, S., & Lohmar, B. (2003). Dynamics of agricultural competitiveness: Policy lessons from abroad. Amber Waves: The Economics of Food, Farming, Natural Resources, and Rural America.
5. https://www.foodformzansi.co.za/explore-the-intricate-web-of-agricultural-market-dynamics.
6. https://www.insightsonindia.com/agriculture/farm-subsidies-and-msp/challenges-and-problems-associated-with-msp.
7. Lencucha, R., Pal, N. E., Appau, A., Thow, A. M., and Drope, J. (2020). Government Policy and Agricultural Production: A Scoping Review to Inform Research and Policy on Healthy Agricultural Commodities. Globalization and health, 16(1), 11.
8. OECD 2013 Draft Framework: Analysing Policies to Improve Agriculture Productivity Growth, Sustainably OECD Publishing.
9. Chintapalli, P., and Tang, C. S. (2022). The Impact of Crop Minimum Support Price on Crop Production and Farmer Welfare. Agricultural Supply Chain Management Research: Operations and Analytics in Planting, Selling, and Government Interventions, 247-264.
10. Chintapalli, P., and Tang, C. S. (2022). The implications of crop minimum support price in the presence of myopic and strategic farmers. European Journal of Operational Research, 300(1), 336-349.
11. Srinivasa, A. K., Praveen, K. V., Padmaja, S. S., Nithyashree, M. L., and Jha, G. K. (2023). Does a farmer's knowledge of minimum support price (MSP) affect the farm-gate price? Evidence from India. Journal of Economics and Development, 25(4), 302-316.
12. https://www.linkedin.com/pulse/exploring-dimensions-agriculture-minimum-support-price-gujral-ojmwc.
13. https://moderndiplomacy.eu/2023/05/17/evaluating-the-impact-of-minimum-support-price-msp-on-agricultural-productivity-and-efficiency/.
14. https://www.linkedin.com/pulse/decoding-indias-msp-policy-impact-farmers-markets-food-forum-0jrvf.
15. https://www.indiainfoline.com/knowledge-center/tax-saving-tax-planning/what-is-minimum-support-price-msp-and-does-it-really-benefit-farmers.
16. https://www.linkedin.com/pulse/exploring-dimensions-agriculture-minimum-support-price-gujral-ojmwc.
17. https://www.linkedin.com/pulse/decoding-indias-msp-policy-impact-farmers markets-food-forum-0jrvf.
18. Bontkes, T. S., and van Keulen, H. (2003). Modelling the dynamics of agricultural development at farm and regional level. Agricultural Systems, 76(1), 379-396.
19. Chavas, J. P., Chambers, R. G., and Pope, R. D. (2010). Production economics and farm management: a century of contributions. American Journal of Agricultural Economics, 92(2), 356-375.

4

Economic Reforms Liberalization Privatization and Globalization

Yellagandula Mani and Mahima Priyanka Neerugatti

Acharya Narendra Deva University of Agriculture and Technology, Kumarganj Ayodhya, Uttar Pradesh

Abstract

Economic reforms encompassing liberalization, privatization, and globalization have been pivotal in shaping the modern economic landscape. This abstract explores the interconnectedness and impact of these reforms on various aspects of economies worldwide. Liberalization refers to the loosening of government controls and regulations on economic activities, facilitating greater competition and market efficiency. It entails the removal of barriers to trade and investment, thereby fostering economic growth and innovation. However, it also poses challenges such as increased inequality and vulnerability to external shocks. Privatization involves the transfer of state-owned enterprises into private hands, aiming to enhance efficiency, productivity, and accountability. By subjecting formerly monopolized sectors to market forces, privatization seeks to improve resource allocation and stimulate economic dynamism. Yet, it raises concerns about social equity, job security, and the concentration of wealth. Globalization denotes the increasing interconnectedness of economies through trade, investment, and technological advancement. It promotes the free flow of goods, capital, and ideas across borders, enabling countries to specialize in their comparative advantages and access wider markets. Nevertheless, globalization can exacerbate disparities between developed and developing nations, fuelling economic volatility and cultural homogenization. Collectively, these reforms have reshaped economic structures, driving rapid economic growth in some regions while exposing vulnerabilities and inequities in others. The pursuit of liberalization, privatization, and globalization requires careful consideration of their socio-economic implications and the implementation of complementary policies to mitigate adverse effects and ensure inclusive development.

Keywords: *Globalization, liberalization, market efficiency, privatization and socio-economic implications*

Introduction

In recent decades, economic reforms centred around liberalization, privatization, and globalization have emerged as fundamental drivers of economic transformation on a global scale. These reforms represent a departure from traditional state-centric economic models, emphasizing market-oriented approaches and greater integration into the global economy. This introduction sets the stage for a deeper exploration of the interconnectedness and impact of these reforms on economies worldwide, highlighting their significance in shaping the contemporary economic landscape.

Historical Background

During the 1980s, India found itself facing an economic crisis characterized by a gradual decline in its economy. By the decade's end in 1990, the country was plunged into a severe Balance of Payments (BOP) crisis. This crisis was caused by a mounting fiscal deficit and escalating overvaluation of the currency. Compounding matters, the invasion of Kuwait by Iraq occurred in the same year, triggering a significant spike in oil prices and a corresponding drop in remittances from Indian expatriate workers. The resultant increase in the cost of purchasing oil and the rapid decrease in net factor income from abroad exacerbated India's economic woes.

Furthermore, the uncertain political situation in India exacerbated the situation. Within a span of just one and a half years, the country saw three different Prime Ministers: Vishwanath Pratap Singh (December 1989 – November 1990), Chandra Shekhar (November 1990 – June 1991), and P. V. Narasimha Rao (June 1991 – May 1996). This political instability meant that there were no cohesive strategies in place to address the economic crisis. Consequently, India sought assistance from the International Monetary Fund (IMF) and the World Bank for emergency loans. However, obtaining this lending was contingent upon meeting certain conditions, primarily focused on implementing structural reforms to revive the economy.

Under the leadership of Prime Minister P. V. Narasimha Rao and then-Finance Minister Dr. Manmohan Singh, an industrial policy that sought to eliminate obstacles impeding industrial expansion was declared revolutionary. The purpose of the 1991 New Economic Policy was to stabilize the economy and implement structural changes. The assortment of fiscal reforms and inflation control strategies that constituted stabilization measures are short-term policies. Long-term policies in nature, structural measures have a profound and enduring impact on the economy. As enumerated by Kumar (2022), these encompassed liberalization, privatization, and globalization. We shall thoroughly examine these.

1991, Economic reforms

Economic policy: Economic policy refers to the actions that governments take in the economic field. It covers the systems for setting levels of taxation, government budgets, the money supply and interest rates as well as the labour market, national ownership, and many other areas of government interventions into the economy.

Economic reforms, 1991: The reform strategy implemented in India in July 1991 encompassed a dual approach of macroeconomic stabilization and structural adjustment. This comprehensive strategy aimed to address both short-term imperatives and long-term goals. In the short term, the focus was on stabilizing the economy to rectify balance of payments issues and curb inflation. Simultaneously, there was an emphasis on restructuring institutions to ensure sustainable growth and development in the long term. An initiative to stabilize the macroeconomy via fiscal correction was expeditiously implemented by the new administration. Trade, industry, and the public sector also underwent structural reforms that were implemented concurrently.

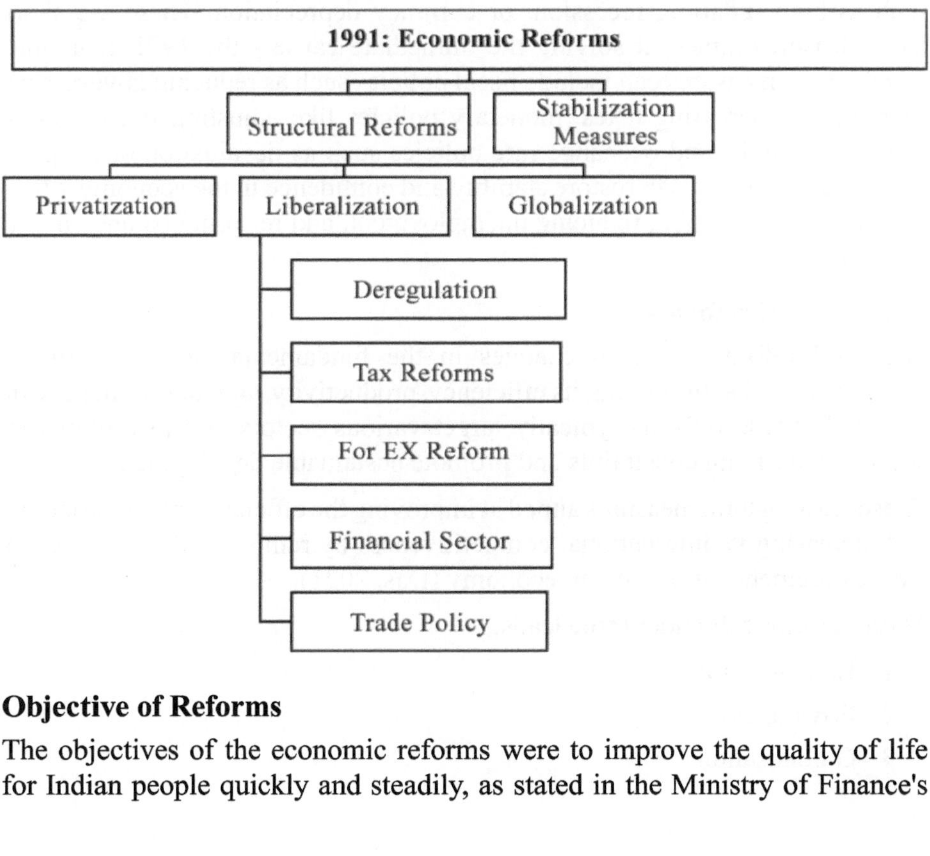

Objective of Reforms

The objectives of the economic reforms were to improve the quality of life for Indian people quickly and steadily, as stated in the Ministry of Finance's

Discussion Paper on Economic Reforms published in July 1993. The swift increase in earnings and gainful employment is essential to achieving this aim. Sustained growth in earnings and employment is the only long-term remedy for the curse of poverty. Investment is necessary for this kind of growth, including in agriculture, roads, irrigation, industry, power, and most importantly, people. It also needs to be a profitable investment. The productivity of our labour, land, and capital must continue to rise for development to be successful and long-lasting.

Major Steps in the 1991 Reforms

The key policy measures implemented by the Government to address the fundamental challenges of the balance of payments issue and structural inflexibilities were as follows:

1. Stabilization measures

Stabilization measures refer to policies implemented by governments or central banks to stabilize an economy, usually during periods of economic instability such as high inflation, recession, or currency depreciation. These are short term measures aimed at solving the immediate cause - the 1991 economic crisis. These measures can include fiscal policies such as reducing government spending or increasing taxes, monetary policies like adjusting interest rates or money supply, and exchange rate policies such as devaluation or pegging currencies. The aim is to restore stability and confidence in the economy, often by controlling inflation, reducing unemployment, and restoring balance in the external sector.

2. Structural reforms

Structural reforms refer to changes in the fundamental structures of an economy aimed at improving its efficiency, productivity, and long-term growth potential. These reforms typically target various sectors and institutions to address underlying constraints and promote sustainable development.

These are long term measures aimed at improving the efficiency of the economy and increasing its international competitiveness by removing the rigidities in various segments of the Indian economy (Das, 2021).

These reforms fall under three leads:

1. Liberalisation
2. Privatisation
3. Globalisation

Liberalisation

Liberalization entails the removal of restrictions, particularly within an economic context. After Independence, the government embraced a protective stance, shielding the economy from external influences. This was motivated by concerns that fledgling domestic industries were not yet robust enough to compete with established international firms, potentially leading to their displacement.

The onset of liberalization signified the conclusion of this era. India embarked on a gradual opening of its economic borders to other nations by easing restrictions. This shift also facilitated foreign investors and the private sector to participate in domestic enterprises. Consequently, it ushered in a free-market system characterized by diminished governmental restrictions and intervention.

Objectives of liberalization

- Economic boundaries were opened to assess the competitiveness of domestic firms.
- Because imports were significantly higher than exports, the BOP imbalance needed to be adjusted.
- By permitting the private sector to engage in economic activity, it was also done to unleash the economy's full potential.
- Permitting foreign corporations to establish operations there to support India's economic expansion.

Examples

- China's Economic Liberalization in 1978, Brazil's Economic Liberalization in 1990, and India's Economic Liberalization in 1991.

Various Sectors of Liberalization

Liberalisation was done in various sectors in the following ways:

1. Deregulation of Industrial Sectors

Industrial Policy Reforms: Several changes were made to the Industrial Policy in order to strengthen the advancements made during the 1980s and to give the home industry more competitive support. On July 24, 1991, the government unveiled the New Industrial Policy. To encourage the development of an industrial economy that is more competitive and efficient, the New Industrial Policy, which was created in 1991, aimed to deregulate industry significantly. The following were the main components of the industrial policy reforms:

- All projects were free from the need for industrial licensing, except for eighteen industries: explosives, hazardous chemicals, alcohol, cigarettes, and drugs.
- A lot of industries that were formerly designated for the public sector are now "deserved." The only things reserved for the public sector are railroads, defence hardware, and nuclear power generating.
- The prices have been left up to the market.
- The requirement for prior clearance from major corporations for capacity expansion or diversification was removed with the abolition of the Monopolies & Restrictive Trade Practices (MRTP) Act.
- The public sector's designated areas were reduced, and the private sector was allowed to participate more in core and fundamental industries. The number of spaces reserved was lowered from 17 to 8 under the new strategy. These eight mostly deal with security and strategic issues. (For instance, atomic energy, railroads, etc.)
- The program promoted the government's disinvestment of its equity share capital holdings in public sector companies.

A Memorandum of Understanding (MOU) between the business and the relevant Ministry set targets for the business to meet, giving the public sector units more autonomy and professional management that could be useful for making reasonable profits.

2. Financial sector Reforms

- Financial Sector reforms aimed at doing away with interest rate distortions and rationalizing the structure of lending rates.
- The transformation of the RBI's role from regulator to a facilitator within the financial sector marked a significant shift in banking reforms.
- These changes paved the way for the emergence of private banks, coinciding with an increase in the cap for FDI in banks to 50%. Despite this transition, certain managerial responsibilities remained under the purview of the RBI, ensuring protection for account holders' interests.
- Interest Rate Liberalisation represented another pivotal aspect of reform. Previously, the RBI dictated rates on deposits and loans, adjusting them based on various factors. However, a phased approach was adopted to deregulate interest rates on deposits, initially focusing on longer-term deposits before extending liberalisation to shorter ones.
- The liberalisation efforts fostered heightened competition among public, private, and foreign banks, dismantling administrative barriers.

Concurrently, reforms in bank branch licensing policies aimed to streamline the branch network, granting banks the flexibility to relocate branches and establish specialized ones.

- Further, guidelines were established for the establishment of new private sector banks, aligning with recommendations from the Narasimham Committee Report. Additionally, updated accounting norms were introduced, refining asset classification and bad debt provisions to enhance transparency and accountability within the banking sector.

3. Tax Reforms

Tax reforms can encompass a wide range of changes to a country's tax system, aiming to improve fairness, simplicity, efficiency, and revenue generation. Here are a few areas often considered in tax reform discussions:

- **Income Tax**: Adjustments to tax brackets, rates, deductions, and credits can make the income tax system more equitable. This may involve raising or lowering tax rates for different income levels, closing loopholes, or simplifying the tax code.
- **Corporate Tax**: Reforms in corporate taxation may involve changing tax rates, closing loopholes, or modifying the treatment of multinational corporations to ensure they pay their fair share of taxes. Governments often seek to balance competitiveness with the need for revenue.

  Corporate tax, which was very high earlier, has been gradually reduced. The tax procedures have been simplified and the rates also have been lowered. 1973-74 - Eleven tax slabs, with rates from 10 to 85 per cent. 1990-91 - In five Budgets between 1991-96, FM Manmohan Singh reduces IT slabs to three (20, 30 and 40 per cent).
- **Sales Tax/VAT**: Changes to consumption taxes, like sales tax or value-added tax (VAT), can impact consumer behaviour and government revenue. Reform efforts may focus on broadening the tax base, adjusting rates, or exempting certain goods or services.
- **Property Tax**: Property tax reforms might involve reassessing property values, adjusting tax rates, or implementing exemptions or relief programs for homeowners, particularly to address issues of affordability and fairness.
- **Wealth Tax**: Some jurisdictions consider implementing a wealth tax on high-net-worth individuals or large estates to address wealth inequality and generate revenue. Such reforms often face debates over practicality and economic impact.

- **Tax Administration**: Improving tax administration processes, including compliance measures, enforcement, and the use of technology, can enhance the efficiency and effectiveness of tax collection while reducing opportunities for tax evasion or fraud.
- **Environmental Taxes**: Governments may introduce or adjust taxes on activities that generate negative externalities, such as carbon emissions or waste production, to incentivize more sustainable behaviour and fund environmental initiatives.
- **International Taxation**: Addressing issues related to cross-border tax avoidance and evasion, including through transfer pricing rules, tax treaties, and efforts to combat tax havens, is crucial for ensuring a fair and equitable global tax system.
- **Social Security and Medicare**: Reforms to funding mechanisms for social security, healthcare, and other social safety net programs may involve changes to payroll taxes, benefit structures, or eligibility criteria to ensure long-term sustainability.

4. Foreign Exchange Reforms

In the post-reform era, the government implemented several significant measures to encourage foreign investment in India. These included:

- The establishment of the Foreign Investment Promotion Board (FIPB) in 1991, which was tasked with negotiating with foreign companies and approving direct foreign investment in specific sectors.
- Periodic actions to encourage foreign institutional investment (FII) in India; and
- The announcement of a specified list of high technology and high-investment priority industries, for which automatic permission was granted for foreign direct investment (FDI) up to 51 percent foreign equity. Over time, the limit was raised to 74 percent and eventually to 100 percent for many of these industries.

5. Trade and Investment Policy Reforms

Under trade policy reforms, the main focus was on greater openness. Hence, the policy package was essentially an outward-oriented one. New initiatives were taken in trade policy to create an environment which would provide a stimulus to export while at the same time reducing the degree of regulation and licensing control on foreign trade. The main feature of the new trade policy as it has evolved over the years since 1991 are as follows:

- **Freer imports and exports:** Prior to 1991, in India imports were regulated by means of a positive list of freely importable items. From 1992, imports were regulated by a limited negative list. For instance, the trade policy of 1 April 1992, freed imports of almost all intermediate and capital goods. Only 71 items remained restricted. Dismantling of quantitative restrictions on imports.
- **Rationalization of tariff structure and removal of quantitative restrictions:** The Chelliah Committee's Report had suggested significant reduction in import duties. It had suggested a peak rate of 50 percent. As a first step towards a gradual reduction in the tariffs, the 1991-92 budget had reduced the peak rate of import duty from more than 300 percent to 150 percent. The process of lowering the customs tariffs was carried further in successive budgets.
- **Trading houses:** The 1991 policy allowed export houses and trading houses to import a wide range of items. The Government also permitted the setting up of trading houses with 51 percent foreign equity for the purpose of promoting exports. For instance, under the 1992-97 trade policy, export houses and trading houses were provided the benefit of self-certification under the advance license system, which permits duty free imports for exports.
- Removal of licensing procedures for imports except in case of hazardous and environmentally sensitive products.
- Quantitative restriction on imports was also fully decreased later.
- Export duties have been removed to promote exports.

Impact of Liberalization on the Economy

The economy experienced a mixed impact following liberalization, with both positive and negative outcomes.

Positive Effects

- **Capital Flow:** Initiatives such as the removal of trade barriers and tax reforms facilitated the unrestricted movement of capital within the economy. This encouraged both domestic and foreign investors to inject funds, fostering overall capital expansion.
- **Diversification of Investor Portfolios:** Eliminating restrictions allowed investors to diversify their portfolios across various asset classes. The expanded investment options attracted investors to spread their resources, thereby reducing investment risk.

- **Stock Market Growth:** The influx of investors and foreign capital contributed to the expansion of the stock market, driving its growth trajectory.

Negative Effects

- **Intensified Competition:** The emergence of private enterprises and multinational corporations intensified competition, posing challenges for small traders who struggled to keep pace with technological advancements resulting from liberalization.
- **Mergers and Acquisitions:** Large private entities gained the ability to acquire majority stakes in smaller firms. Consequently, employees of these smaller companies faced job losses unless they could acquire the necessary skills to retain their positions.

Privatisation

Previously, India operated under a socialist framework, where state-owned enterprises played a dominant role in the economy. The government-controlled prices and regulated various sectors to ensure social welfare and affordability, given the country's economic challenges. However, with the advent of liberalization, there arose a need to shift away from this model. Alongside liberalization, privatization emerged as a key strategy.

Privatization involves transferring ownership, management, and control of public sector companies from the government to private entities. This process is also known as disinvestment, as it often involves selling off shares of state-owned companies, essentially the reverse of investment (Ghosh, 2021). Privatization can occur through outright sales of public sector companies or through gradual disinvestment initiatives.

Examples

Some of the examples of PSUs that were privatized include-Bharat Aluminium Company Limited (BALCO), Hindustan Zinc Limited (HZL), and Hotel Corporation of India Limited (HCI).

Objectives of Privatization

The objectives of privatization encompassed several key aims:

- **Reducing Government Control:** Privatization aimed to diminish government control over various industries, allowing for greater autonomy and decision-making authority within the private sector.
- **Fundraising through Disinvestment:** Privatisation of public sector enterprises by selling off part of the equity of PSEs to the public is called

Disinvestment. By selling off stakes in Public Sector Undertakings (PSUs), privatization sought to raise funds for the government, providing financial resources for other priorities or investments.

- **Reducing Government Workload:** Privatization aimed to alleviate the administrative burden on the government by transferring the management and operation of enterprises to the private sector, reducing direct government involvement in day-to-day operations.
- **Enhancing Management Autonomy:** Privatization aimed to empower the management of PSUs with increased autonomy, enabling them to make strategic decisions independently of government bureaucracy and political interference.
- **Promoting Competition and Efficiency:** By fostering a more competitive environment among firms, privatization aimed to enhance efficiency, innovation, and productivity within industries, ultimately benefiting consumers and the economy.

Types of Privatization

There are four types of privatization. These include:

- **Complete Privatization:** This involves the outright sale of government assets to the private sector, including the transfer of management control of Public Sector Undertakings (PSUs).
- **Privatization of Operations:** Here, managerial, and operational responsibilities of PSUs are transferred to private firms, which utilize government assets to generate revenue. An example is sports leagues using government-owned stadiums.
- **Contracting Out:** Under this approach, the government pays private sector firms for specific services rendered.
- **Open Competition:** In this type, private firms compete within governmental jurisdiction. An illustration of this is observed in the telecom sector.

In India, a combination of complete privatization, open competition, and contracting was used to achieve the goal of privatization.

Impact of Privatization

Positive Impacts

- **Government Burden Reduction:** Privatization alleviates the government's burden by shifting its focus away from managing numerous companies, allowing it to concentrate efforts on other vital areas.

- **Enhanced Decision-Making:** Granting greater autonomy to managers fosters better decision-making skills, potentially leading to more effective management practices.
- **Revival of Troubled Units:** Transferring ownership, management, and control to private entities facilitates the restructuring of struggling Public Sector Undertakings (PSUs), increasing the likelihood of their recovery.

Negative Impacts

- **Monopoly Risks:** Dominance by major private players can pose risks of monopolistic control, as they may have the resources to acquire competing firms, reducing market competition.
- **Diminished Welfare Initiatives:** Unlike the public sector, the private sector is not obligated to prioritize public welfare. Consequently, private firms may focus solely on profit-making activities, potentially neglecting the needs of underprivileged populations.

Globalisation

The Indian government's previous policy of maintaining a closed economy isolated the country from the global market. To foster the involvement of foreign enterprises, the next logical step was to integrate India's economy with the global economy.

Globalization entails the integration of a nation's economy with the global economy, aiming to create a borderless world where goods, services, and people can move freely across borders. This integration has been facilitated by advancements in technology, enabling connectivity between people worldwide. Globalization represents the culmination of the liberalization and privatization efforts, allowing multinational corporations to establish manufacturing and retail operations within the country and enabling domestic firms to expand internationally (Chakrabarti, 2021).

India became a member of the World Trade Organization (WTO) in January 1995. Under WTO regulations, member countries are assured fair treatment of their exports by other members, and they reciprocate with equitable treatment of imports. As a signatory to the General Agreement on Tariffs and Trade (GATT), the precursor to the WTO, India committed to actions promoting trade liberalization. Embracing the motto of free trade, member nations, including India, endeavoured to globalize their economies by reducing tariffs on various goods. This initiative aimed to level the playing field for developing countries competing with their developed counterparts in the global market.

In 1991, globalization was formally embraced as a reform measure in India. This included the removal of trade restrictions to facilitate smoother export and import processes, signalling a significant shift towards greater economic openness and engagement with the global marketplace.

Objectives of Globalization

- One of the main objectives was to reduce customs duties and tariffs. This was done to ease the importing and exporting of goods. Fewer taxes meant that companies could import materials or products at cheaper rates.
- Removal of restrictions on foreign trade was another objective that had to be undertaken.
- Increasing the equity limit for foreign investment was important to let foreign investors invest more in domestic companies.

Impact of Globalization

Positive Impact

- **Outsourcing:** A significant outcome of liberalization was the emergence of outsourcing, where companies hire professionals from other countries to perform tasks at a lower cost. While cost-effectiveness is a key driver, outsourcing is also motivated by access to rare skills found in specific regions. Major services like marketing, legal advice, technical support, and IT often get outsourced. India's inexpensive yet skilled workforce has made it an attractive destination for organizations in developed countries seeking these services.
- **Liberalization of Foreign Exchange Regulations:** The liberalization of the Foreign Exchange Regulation Act (FERA) in 1993, followed by the enactment of the Foreign Exchange Management Act (FEMA) in 1999, facilitated transactions in foreign currency, enabling smoother international trade and investment.

Negative Impacts

- **Disproportionate Growth:** Globalization can lead to uneven economic growth within a country. Regions with well-developed infrastructure conducive to trade tend to benefit the most, resulting in faster growth rates compared to less developed areas. This disparity often prompts migration as people seek better opportunities in economically thriving regions.
- **Increased Competition:** The influx of foreign goods into the domestic market intensifies competition. While competition is generally

considered healthy, excessive competition can negatively impact domestic players, potentially driving them out of the market. This can also have implications for the country's GDP growth.

Effect of Liberalization, Privatization, and Globalization on the Indian Economy

The India we see today has been shaped by strategic decisions made in response to the economic crisis of 1990. These decisions brought about a mixture of positive and negative outcomes, shaping the trajectory of the country's development (Chaudhuri, *et al.*, 2022).

Effect on Different Sectors

1. **Impact on Small-scale Industries:** The liberalization, privatization, and globalization (LPG) policies significantly impacted small-scale industries. Previously, certain items were exclusively reserved for them to manufacture. However, with liberalization, larger private enterprises began producing superior and more affordable alternatives to these goods. Consequently, small-scale industries lost their competitive edge and are now struggling to sustain themselves in the market.
2. **Impact on Agriculture:** The agricultural sector experienced minimal impact following the introduction of these reforms. Approximately 55% of the population remains dependent on agriculture for their livelihoods. Government oversight continues to influence various facets of this sector. Importation of certain agricultural goods into the market contributes to fluctuating commodity prices.
3. **Impact on the Services Sector:** The LPG reforms brought about substantial gains in various sectors, notably spearheading a technological revolution across the nation. Industries such as IT, banking, stock markets, and telecommunications flourished, creating numerous job opportunities and driving significant GDP growth. The entry of private players injected dynamism into these sectors, leading to their rapid expansion. However, sectors like education and healthcare witnessed comparatively slower growth, drawing criticism due to their essential nature. As these are vital services, the responsibility for welfare activities falls primarily on the government, as private entities prioritize profit over public welfare.

Positive Effects of Liberalization, Privatization, and Globalization (LPG):

- **Increase in GDP Growth Rate:** With the participation of private companies and multinational corporations, India experienced a surge in economic growth. LPG policies attracted foreign direct investment and bolstered forex reserves, laying a robust foundation for both public and private sectors. Consequently, India's GDP growth rate soared to an impressive 8% annually.

- **Growth of Industries:** LPG policies stimulated the growth of industries, both by increasing their numbers and strengthening existing ones. The IT sector witnessed remarkable expansion, attracting numerous multinational companies to establish operations in India and outsource IT-related work to domestic firms.
- **Controlling Inflation:** LPG aimed to curb inflation by addressing the imbalance between demand and supply. Opening the economy facilitated increased money flow and expanded commodity supply, thereby mitigating inflationary pressures.
- **Reducing Fiscal Deficit:** Liberalization eased import and export restrictions, resulting in a boost in exports and a corresponding inflow of dollars. Additionally, rupee devaluation enhanced India's competitiveness in the international market, contributing to a reduction in fiscal deficit.
- **Reducing Poverty:** The proliferation of industrial units created ample job opportunities, leading to increased demand for skilled and unskilled labour. This job growth, coupled with improved standards of living, lifted many people out of poverty, contributing to poverty reduction across the country.

Negative Effects of Liberalization, Privatization, and Globalization (LPG):

- **Uneven Growth:** The agricultural sector was largely neglected during the reform process, resulting in uneven growth across sectors. While support services experienced growth, direct interventions to uplift the agricultural sector were limited, exacerbating disparities in development.
- **Disparity Between Rich and Poor:** Economic growth disproportionately favoured the wealthy, widening the gap between the rich and the poor. While the affluent segment saw substantial improvements in their living standards, many individuals from lower-income groups failed to experience significant benefits from the reforms, leading to a widening wealth gap.
- **Health and Education Sectors:** The health and education sectors did not witness substantial improvements compared to other sectors following the reforms. With the primary focus on economic revival,

social sectors like health and education did not receive adequate attention or investment, hindering their development and perpetuating existing challenges in access and quality of services.

Conclusion

In conclusion, the economic reforms of liberalization, privatization, and globalization (LPG) have profoundly reshaped India's economic landscape. These reforms were initiated to address the challenges posed by the 1990 economic crisis, with the aim of unlocking the country's growth potential, enhancing competitiveness, and integrating into the global economy. Liberalization opened the economy, dismantling barriers to trade and investment, fostering competition, and spurring innovation. Privatization transferred ownership and management of state-owned enterprises to the private sector, promoting efficiency and productivity. Globalization facilitated greater economic integration with the world, enabling the free flow of goods, services, capital, and technology across borders.

The outcomes of these reforms have been mixed. On the positive side, they have led to rapid economic growth, job creation, technological advancement, and increased foreign investment. However, challenges such as growing income inequality, uneven regional development, and environmental degradation have also emerged. Moving forward, it is essential to address these challenges while leveraging the opportunities presented by economic reforms to foster inclusive and sustainable growth. This requires effective governance, investment in human capital and infrastructure, and policies that ensure equitable distribution of the benefits of growth. Overall, the economic reforms of liberalization, privatization, and globalization have been transformative for India, shaping its path towards becoming a global economic powerhouse.

References

Chakrabarti, Rajesh. (2021). "Globalization, privatisation and economic policy: A perspective from India." Cambridge Journal of Economics, 45(5), 1219-1236.

Chaudhuri, Shubhamoy, & Dutta, Meghna. (2022). "Impact of Liberalisation, Privatisation and Globalisation on Indian Economy: An Empirical Study." Journal of Commerce & Management Thought, 13(1), 144-160.

Das, Pranab. (2021). "Liberalisation, Privatisation and Globalisation: A Review of Indian Economy." Indian Journal of Public Administration, 67(2), 229-240.

Ghosh, Jayati. (2021). "Reform or deform? Privatisation and public goods in India." Economic and Political Weekly, 56(24), 12-15.

Kumar, Nagesh. (2022). "Liberalisation, Privatisation and Globalisation: Three Decades On." Economic and Political Weekly, 57(2), 40-46.

New Economic Policy (NEP) 1991 – Indian Economy Notes (prepp.in) https://prepp.in/news/e-492-new-economic-policy-nep-1991-indian-economy-notes

New Economic Policy 1991: Features & New Policy Reforms of NEP (testbook.com) https://testbook.com/ias-preparation

5

The Interplay Between Minimum Support Price (MSP) and Market Forces

Narendra Yadav and Diksha Bohra

Maharana Pratap University of Agriculture & Technology, Udaipur, Rajasthan

Abstract

Agriculture is the backbone of Indian economy. Agriculture sector accounts for 18.8 per cent of GVA in 2021-22. The farmer has been successful in providing food to the increasing population, but the farmer is not able to get a good price for what he produces. That why government of India announced Minimum Support Price (MSP) before sowing the crop on the recommendation of CACP (Commission for Agricultural Cost and Prices). MSP acts as a price floor, meaning it establishes a minimum price at which the government agrees to purchase farmers' crops. MSP provides a safety net for farmers against price fluctuations caused by market forces such as demand-supply dynamics, weather conditions, and international trade factors. While MSP sets a minimum price, market forces still influence the equilibrium price. If market prices rise above the MSP due to factors like increased demand or reduced supply, farmers may sell their produce in the open market rather than to government agencies. Conversely, if market prices fall below the MSP, the government may step in to procure the produce to support farmers, leading to market stabilization. It is conclude that MSP aims to protect farmers, from market volatility and ensure food security and its interplay with market forces is complex. MSP balancing the interests of farmers, consumers, and fiscal constraints requires careful policy design and monitoring to achieve efficient outcomes in agricultural markets.

Keywords: *Agriculture, MSP, Market force, Farmer, Price*

Introduction

Agriculture plays a vital role in India's economy 54.6 per cent of the total workforce was engaged in agricultural and allied sector activities (Census 2011). Agriculture sector is estimated to grow 3.9 per cent in 2021-22 on top of 3.6 per cent and 4.3 per cent, respectively in the previous two years.

Agriculture sector accounts for 18.8 per cent of GVA in 2021-22 (Economic Survey 2021-22). The agricultural industry has experienced numerous issues, such as a shortage of food, because of the high cost of production and low yield per hectare. In certain situations, it has also grown more difficult to provide for their fundamental requirements, such as clothes and shelter. By boosting their income and purchasing power through agricultural inputs like fertilizers, insecticides, agricultural equipment, etc., agricultural marketers in India play a crucial role in the rural areas. The India is world's biggest producer of agricultural goods. Food grain output grew significantly during the 1960s and 1970s, with wheat and rice production rising. Compared to farmers in Western nations, farmers in countries like India, China, and Japan are more prone to growing cash crops.

The Minimum Support Price (MSP) system is a critical component of agricultural policy in many countries, aimed at ensuring farmers receive a fair and stable income for their produce. However, the relationship between MSP and market forces is complex, as MSP policies can impact agricultural markets, farmer livelihoods, government budgets, and food security. This chapter explores the interplay between MSP and market forces, examining the challenges, benefits, and implications of MSP policies in the context of agricultural markets.

Minimum Support Price (MSP): Minimum Support Price (MSP) is the price set by the government before sowing the crop to provide a safety net to farmers for their agricultural produce, ensuring them a minimum guaranteed price for their crops. MSP considers factors such as input costs, market prices, and demand-supply dynamics. MSP also known as price floor, it is announced by government of India on the recommendation of CACP (Commission for Agricultural Cost and Prices) that was came into existence in January 1965. Earlier since 1985, CACP named as Agricultural Prices Commission. CACP submit recommendations to the government in the form of Price Policy reports every year, separately for five groups of commodities namely Kharif crops, Rabi crops, Sugarcane (Fair and remunerative price), Raw Jute and Copra (7 Cereals, 5 Pulses, 8 Oilseed and 4 commercial crops). As per the recommendation of M.S. Swami Nathan Committee (2006) the union budget for 2018-19 had announced that MSP would be kept at levels of 1.5 times of the cost of production (Cost C2 + 50 % of Cost C2).

Objectives of MSP

1. To ensure remunerative prices to the growers for encouraging higher investment and production.

2. Support the farmers from distress sales and to procure food grains for public distribution.
3. MSP also aims to bring a balances realization of sufficient food production and consumption needs.

Market: A market is any collection of individuals or businesses that are willing and able to buy a good or service that fulfils their demands. It is not necessarily limited by geographical boundaries unless we specify those boundaries. It doesn't characterize the individuals or groups in any way other than their desire and capacity for purchase.

Overview of Market Forces in Agriculture: Agricultural markets are influenced by various factors, including supply and demand dynamics, weather conditions, input costs, technological advancements, government policies, trade regulations, and consumer preferences. These market forces can lead to price volatility, income uncertainty for farmers, and fluctuations in food supply and prices.

The combined impact of buyers and sellers on the amount and price of products and services available in a market is represented by the forces of supply and demand. Excessive demand raises both prices and supply quantities, while excessive supply lowers prices. While MSP sets a minimum price, market forces still influence the equilibrium price. If market prices rise above the MSP due to factors like increased demand or reduced supply, farmers may sell their produce in the open market rather than to government agencies. Conversely, if market prices fall below the MSP, the government may step in to procure the produce to support farmers, leading to market stabilization.

Market forces could include seasonality, quantity available, quality requirements, reliability of supply, prices, market manipulations, promotion, market trends, consumer preference, political intervention, exchange rate.

Factor Affecting the Marketing of a Product

- Demand
- Price
- Supply
- Buyer's demographics – age, sex, nation, beliefs, education
- Cultural and social (e.g. fashion, Customer demand):- Culture has a big impact on how consumers view items and how much demand there is for them. Because consumer pressures vary among cultures, marketing or selling a product may not be a feasible option in another. Marketing pork goods to Australia is one way to do this, as opposed to a similar

marketing campaign in a nation like Pakistan. Thorough study is also necessary prior to implementing brand names and logos and promoting them in particular nations. Words and logos can have diverse cultural connotations and occasionally cause offense.

- **Economic Factor:** The demand and supply for a product is affected by:
- Government policy
- Economic conditions of a country
- Trading partners
- Interest rates
- Money supply
- Credit availability
- Inflation
- Price control regulations
- The economic policies of a country are an important market force, especially New Zealand which exports most of its products.
- **Political Factor:** Product marketing sometimes involves political considerations. Marketers must keep an eye on political developments and trends in the nations where their goods are sold, as well as consider the potential effects that shifting political conditions may have on their company.
- **Technological Factor:** The way we live, both personally and professionally, could undergo significant changes because of evolving technology. Since many families now have two working partners, there is less time for home duties. These technological advancements have the potential to quickly build or destroy established companies. This has led to a rise in the market for household appliances that save time, such microwaves. Purchasing food to go is another area where demand has surged due to households seeking time-efficient lifestyle options. In many cases, the traditional "leg of lamb" is being replaced with processed and pre-prepared meals. Additionally, the Internet is having a significant impact on our daily lives. For example, the number of items bought online is rising quickly, placing pressure on some businesses like travel agencies, sales teams, and marketing.
- **Competition:** This is a market force arising from the same, or similar, product under different brand names satisfying the same need or demand. Competition may also arise from completely different products competing for the same market. The marketer must find a way of beating

the competition, and one method is by branding. A brand may simply be a fun sticker such as a cartoon character on an apple to attract the children market.

- **Environmental:** Our capacity to promote our products can be significantly impacted by how foreign consumers view our industry. Animal welfare might affect the market. Customers are choosing to purchase "animal friendly" products consciously and becoming more knowledgeable of the production processes used in products. The company or supplier might have to alter their production processes, which would result in increased expenses. For instance, transport and killing.
- **Global Factor:** India's signing of the GATT agreements in 1994 and her joining the World Trade Organization as a founder member have put Indian agriculture into the framework of global competition and rule of the global market. (Quota, tariffs, trade restrictions, currency exchange rates, disease status).

Impact of MSP on Agricultural Markets

Price Support and Market Distortions: MSP policies aim to provide price stability and income support to farmers, but they can also distort agricultural markets by artificially inflating prices, discouraging private investment, and leading to market inefficiencies. Critics argue that MSPs can create surpluses, distort planting decisions, and hinder the development of competitive market structures.

Farmer Income and Welfare: MSPs play a crucial role in ensuring farmers receive a fair and remunerative price for their produce, thereby improving their income and livelihoods. MSPs provide a safety net during times of price volatility or market failures, reducing the risk of income losses for farmers and promoting agricultural sustainability.

Government Budgetary Implications: The implementation of MSP policies involves significant financial costs for the government, including procurement, storage, and subsidy expenses. MSP operations can strain government budgets, especially in times of bumper harvests or when market prices are below MSP levels. Balancing the need for price support with fiscal sustainability is a key challenge for policymakers.

Strategies for Balancing MSP and Market Forces

Price Discovery Mechanisms: The process of price discovery involves interacting with buyers and sellers to establish market pricing. Often called a price discovery process or price discovery mechanism, price discovery is a process that uses interactions between sellers and buyers to determine the spot price of a product.

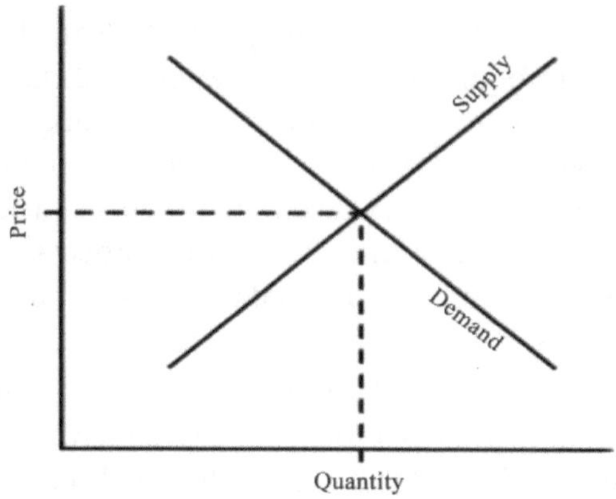

To mitigate market distortions and promote price discovery, policymakers can consider implementing transparent and efficient mechanisms for setting MSPs, such as cost-based pricing, market intelligence systems, and consultation with stakeholders. Additionally, linking MSPs to broader market indicators can help align support prices with market realities.

Market Reforms and Deregulation: Introducing market-oriented reforms, such as liberalizing agricultural markets, promoting contract farming, improving market infrastructure, and encouraging private sector participation, can enhance market efficiency and reduce the reliance on MSPs. Deregulation measures aim to create a competitive and dynamic agricultural sector while ensuring fair returns to farmers.

Targeted Support and Risk Management: Complementing MSPs with targeted support measures, such as crop insurance, income support schemes, agricultural extension services, and investment in rural infrastructure, can enhance farmers' resilience to market shocks and improve their overall well-being. Risk management strategies aim to address the underlying vulnerabilities faced by farmers and mitigate the impact of market fluctuations.

Regular Review Mechanism: Implement a system where MSPs are regularly reviewed and adjusted based on market conditions, production costs, and other relevant factors. This ensures that MSPs remain aligned with market realities.

Transparent Price Discovery: Foster transparency in price discovery mechanisms to ensure that MSPs are reflective of actual market demand and supply dynamics. This can involve the use of technology platforms and market information systems.

Flexibility in MSPs: Provide flexibility in MSPs to account for variations in regional production costs, quality of produce, and market demand. This can involve differential pricing mechanisms based on geographical factors.

Crop Diversification Incentives: Offer incentives for crop diversification to reduce the dependency on MSP-supported crops. This helps in mitigating market distortions caused by excessive reliance on MSPs for specific crops.

Market Intelligence and Forecasting: Invest in market intelligence and forecasting systems to anticipate demand-supply imbalances and adjust MSPs accordingly. This proactive approach helps in minimizing the need for sudden MSP interventions.

Encourage Private Sector Participation: Facilitate private sector involvement in agricultural markets to introduce competition and efficiency. This can complement MSPs by providing farmers with alternative marketing channels and price discovery mechanisms.

Risk Management Tools: Provide farmers with access to risk management tools such as crop insurance and price hedging mechanisms. This empowers farmers to manage market risks more effectively, reducing their dependence on MSPs.

Strengthening Market Infrastructure: Invest in the development of agricultural infrastructure such as storage facilities, transportation networks, and market yards. This enhances market efficiency and reduces post-harvest losses, thereby exerting less pressure on MSPs.

Promote Farmer Producer Organizations (FPOs): Support the formation and strengthening of FPOs to enable collective bargaining power for farmers. FPOs can negotiate better prices in the market, reducing the need for MSP support.

Gradual MSP Reduction: Implement a gradual reduction strategy for MSPs for crops that have achieved market stability. This phased approach allows markets to adjust gradually while providing farmers with time to adapt to changing price dynamics.

Neutralizing the Impact of Market Forces

Our agribusiness is constantly impacted by market pressures; therefore managers and operators may need to think about ways to mitigate these consequences.

Diversification: Agriculture Diversification refers to either a change in cropping pattern or the farmers opting for other non-farming options like poultry farming, animal husbandry, etc. This practice allows farmers to expand the production, which helps generate a higher level of income.

Modifying Production Targets: Modifying production targets as demand increases or decreases.

Environmental Issues: Targeting specific markets requires careful consideration of decisions about the use of chemicals and genetic modification. For example, any decisions about genetically modified organisms (GM) or chemical residues in products must be weighed against the potential danger of disease or pests if organic and non-GE markets are to be addressed. Production decisions will also be impacted by nutrient input limitations. Phosphate and nitrogen.

Investment: Additional investment in some areas of the business may be required to maintain market share. I.e., Research and development, production technology. Many primary industries pay a levy to fund research and development.

Concerns Regarding Animal Welfare: Modifying husbandry practices to take market sentiment into account.

Markets of Interest: A sector of the economy that focuses mostly on one market might have to think about branching out. Some might have to think about cutting back or shifting their target markets.

Supply timing: When a product is going to be supplied to the market.

Conclusion

The interplay between Minimum Support Price (MSP) and market forces in agriculture is multifaceted, with implications for farmers, consumers, governments, and the broader economy. While MSP policies provide essential income support to farmers and ensure food security, they can also distort agricultural markets and strain government budgets. Balancing the objectives of price stability, farmer welfare, and market efficiency requires a nuanced approach that considers the dynamic nature of agricultural markets and the diverse needs of stakeholders.

References

Barrett, C. B. (2020). "Agricultural Markets and Development: A Brief Review of the Literature." Annual Review of Resource Economics, 12, 421–439.

Dhankhar, J. N. (2009). Futures Market in Indian Agriculture and Its Impact on Production and Prices. Indian Journal of Agricultural Economics, 64(3).

Geetha, R. S., & Mahesh, V. (2019). Minimum support prices (MSP) and its influence on cotton farming in India. Asian Journal of Agricultural Extension, Economics & Sociology, 30(4), 1-8.

Gulati, A., & Saini, S. (2018). "Agricultural Price Policy, Farm Profitability, and Food Security: Emerging Markets Perspective." Indian Journal of Agricultural Economics, 73(3), 281–292.

Gupta, R. K., Kumar, V., Singh, P. K., Danish, M., & Dehariya, N. (2020). Impact of minimum support price on agricultural production in Western India. International Journal of Current Microbiology and Applied Sciences, 9(6), 2291-2303.

Kumar, D., & Sekher, M. (2023). Minimum Support Price and the Changing Nature of Rural Economy and Its Implications on Agriculture in Haryana. Business Perspectives and Research, 22785337231164205.

Niti Aayog 2016.

Shiva, V. (2016). "The Violence of the Green Revolution: Third World Agriculture, Ecology, and Politics." Lexington Books.

Sucha Singh Gill, & Jaswinder Singh Brar. (1996). Global Market and Competitiveness of Indian Agriculture: Some Issues. Economic and Political Weekly, 31(32), 2167–2177. http://www.jstor.org/stable/4404499.

Swinnen, J. (2021). "Agricultural Price Intervention and Market Integration." American Journal of Agricultural Economics, 103(2), 605–631.

Vanshika, S., & Harsana, P. (2022). Minimum support price conundrum and sustainable farming: a study of the impact of the socio-economic factors on sustainable agriculture. Vantage J Them Anal.

World Bank. (2019). "Growing Food for Growing Cities: Transforming Food Systems in an Urbanizing World." Washington, DC: World Bank.

6

Deciphering Economic Policies Fiscal Measures and Beyond

Harshit Mishra[1], Ankit Tiwari[2] and Deepchand Nishad[3]

[1]Dept. of Agricultural Economics, College of Agriculture, Acharya Narendra Deva University of Agriculture and Technology, Kumarganj, Ayodhya, Uttar Pradesh

[2]Dept. of Agricultural Economics, College of Agriculture, Acharya Narendra Deva University of Agriculture and Technology, Kumarganj, Ayodhya, Uttar Pradesh

[3]Dept. of Agricultural Economics, College of Agriculture, Acharya Narendra Deva University of Agriculture and Technology, Kumarganj, Ayodhya, Uttar Pradesh

Abstract

Financial markets act as the circulatory system of a healthy economy, channelling capital and liquidity. A 2023 World Bank report estimates that global financial assets reached a staggering $535 trillion, highlighting their immense scale. These markets connect those with surplus funds (savers, investors) to those needing capital (businesses, governments). This fuels business growth, job creation and ultimately, economic prosperity. Fiscal policy, a major partner to financial markets, utilizes government spending, taxation and borrowing to achieve economic goals. The International Monetary Fund (IMF) emphasizes its objectives as promoting economic growth, maintaining price stability (around 2-3% inflation) and achieving a fair distribution of income. Governments can use expansionary spending on infrastructure or social programs to stimulate economic activity during downturns. Conversely, contractionary spending with tax increases helps control inflation during economic booms. Taxation also influences behaviour, with environmental taxes, for example, encouraging greener practices. However, navigating this policy space requires careful consideration of national debt, a measure of government borrowing and ensuring fiscal sustainability for future generations. Beyond fiscal measures, monetary policy plays a important role. Central banks, like the US Federal Reserve, influence interest rates and credit availability to achieve economic stability. Trade policy, encompassing free trade agreements or protectionist measures, significantly impacts economic growth and job markets. Finally, well-designed regulations balance market efficiency with public interest, as with environmental regulations or anti-trust laws. Evaluating the effectiveness *of economic policies can be challenging. Metrics like Gross Domestic Product (GDP), unemployment rate and inflation rate provide a snapshot of economic health. However, isolating the impact of a single policy amidst time lags and other economic factors requires careful analysis. Transparency and accountability in policymaking are crucial for navigating this complex landscape.*

Keywords: *Economic Growth, Financial Markets, Fiscal Policy, Monetary Policy, Regulation*

Introduction

Financial markets play a critical role in the health and stability of a nation's economy. They act as a complex network where individuals, businesses and governments can exchange financial instruments, facilitating the flow of capital and fostering economic growth. According to the World Bank, the global stock market capitalization reached a staggering $93 trillion USD in 2022, highlighting the vast pool of resources circulating within these systems. At the heart of financial markets lies the ability to connect those who possess capital with those who require it (Karpova *et al.,* 2020). Companies seeking to expand their operations can raise funds by issuing stocks or bonds, essentially selling a piece of ownership or a promise to repay a loan with interest. Investors, on the other hand, can utilize these markets to put their money to work, seeking returns on their investments through dividends, interest payments, or capital appreciation. This efficient allocation of resources fuels economic growth by enabling businesses to invest, innovate and create jobs.

Fiscal policy, a cornerstone of economic management, stands as a crucial tool for governments to influence financial markets and the broader economy. This policy framework encompasses three primary instruments: government spending, taxation and government borrowing. By strategically increasing or decreasing spending on infrastructure, social programs and other areas, governments can stimulate economic activity during downturns or curb inflation during periods of overheating. Taxation, another key lever, allows governments to raise revenue to finance spending and influence behaviour. Governments can implement progressive tax structures where higher earners contribute a larger share, or they can utilize targeted tax breaks to incentivize specific activities like research and development. Finally, governments can resort to borrowing when necessary, issuing bonds to raise funds for various purposes. While national debt plays a crucial role in enabling governments to invest in long-term projects, maintaining fiscal sustainability is vital to ensure the long-term health of the economy (Anderson *et al.,* 2023).

Beyond the realm of fiscal policy, other factors significantly impact financial markets. Monetary policy, spearheaded by central banks, plays a critical role in influencing economic activity through interest rates and credit availability. Central banks can raise interest rates to curb inflation and slow economic growth or lower them to stimulate borrowing and investment. Effective coordination between fiscal and monetary policy is essential to achieve economic stability. Trade policy, another major player, dictates how openly a country interacts with the global marketplace. Free trade agreements aim to eliminate barriers and promote economic growth through increased trade, while protectionist policies seek to shield domestic industries from foreign competition. The appropriate balance between these approaches depends on a nation's specific economic circumstances (Amores *et al.,* 2023).

Regulatory policy also plays a vital role in shaping financial markets. Governments must strike a delicate balance between fostering market efficiency and safeguarding public interests. Regulations can encompass environmental standards to promote sustainability, or anti-trust laws to prevent monopolies from stifling competition. A well-designed regulatory framework ensures fair play within financial markets, fostering trust and stability.

Evaluating the effectiveness of economic policies is an ongoing challenge. Important metrics like Gross Domestic Product (GDP), which measures the total value of goods and services produced within a country, serve as primary indicators of economic health. The unemployment rate and inflation rate are also crucial gauges, reflecting the state of the labour market and price stability, respectively (Chugunov *et al.,* 2021). However, pinpointing the exact impact of a single policy can be challenging due to time lags and the complex interplay of various factors influencing the economy. Transparency and accountability within the policymaking process are paramount to ensure that economic interventions deliver on their intended outcomes.

Financial markets serve as the backbone of modern economies, facilitating the allocation of capital and driving economic growth. Governments and institutions actively influence these markets through fiscal, monetary, trade and regulatory policies. By carefully calibrating these instruments, policymakers strive to achieve economic stability, promote growth, and ensure a fair and sustainable financial system. Understanding the intricate dynamics of these policies and their impact on financial markets is essential for navigating the ever-evolving global economic landscape (Romer, 2021).

Demystifying Fiscal Policy

Fiscal policy stands as a cornerstone in the arsenal of economic tools wielded by governments to navigate the tumultuous waters of economic activity. It embodies the strategic manoeuvring of government expenditures, taxation regimes and borrowing practices to sculpt the trajectory of a nation's economy. Underpinning its complexity lies a framework designed to address various macroeconomic objectives, from stimulating growth to ensuring equitable wealth distribution. Let us embark on a journey to unravel the intricacies of fiscal policy.

Definition and Scope

At its core, fiscal policy encompasses the decisions and actions undertaken by governments pertaining to revenue generation, expenditure allocation and debt management. These actions manifest through three primary channels:

a. **Government Spending:** Government spending represents the financial outlays directed towards an array of public goods and services. These expenditures encompass investments in infrastructure, education, healthcare, defence, and myriad other sectors vital for societal well-being and economic advancement. Through judicious allocation, governments endeavour to stimulate demand, foster employment opportunities and bolster overall economic activity.

b. **Taxation:** Taxation emerges as a fundamental pillar of fiscal policy, serving as the conduit through which governments garner revenue to fund public expenditures. Taxes assume various forms, ranging from income and corporate taxes to sales and excise duties. The imposition and alteration of tax policies wield significant influence over consumer behaviour, business decisions and overall economic performance. By modulating tax rates and structures, governments seek to incentivize investment, spur consumption, and achieve redistribution goals.

c. **Government Borrowing:** In scenarios where expenditures surpass revenue, governments resort to borrowing to bridge the fiscal deficit. Bond issuance and debt accumulation constitute primary mechanisms through which governments procure funds from domestic and international sources. While borrowing enables governments to finance critical initiatives and sustain expenditure levels, it also engenders implications for fiscal sustainability, interest rates and intergenerational equity. Prudent debt management practices are imperative to forestall adverse repercussions on economic stability and investor confidence (Postula and Radecka-Moroz, 2020).

Objectives of Fiscal Policy

The pursuit of fiscal policy is underpinned by a triad of overarching objectives, each wielding profound implications for economic performance and societal welfare:

a. **Promoting Economic Growth:** Central among the objectives of fiscal policy is the stimulation of robust and sustainable economic growth. By fostering an environment conducive to investment, innovation and productivity enhancements, governments endeavour to catalyse expansionary forces within the economy. Strategic deployment of fiscal measures, such as infrastructure development and investment incentives, aims to bolster aggregate demand, stimulate private sector activity, and propel long-term growth trajectories.

b. **Maintaining Price Stability:** Price stability stands as a linchpin of macroeconomic stability, fostering predictability and confidence within the economy. Fiscal policy plays a pivotal role in mitigating inflationary pressures and deflationary risks through judicious demand management and supply-side interventions. By calibrating expenditure levels and taxation policies, governments seek to temper fluctuations in aggregate demand and uphold price stability, thereby safeguarding purchasing power and fostering optimal resource allocation.

c. **Achieving Equitable Distribution of Income:** Amidst the pursuit of economic prosperity, fiscal policy assumes a redistributive mandate aimed at fostering social cohesion and equitable access to opportunities. Through progressive taxation, targeted welfare programs and investment in human capital, governments endeavour to narrow socioeconomic disparities and engender inclusive growth. By addressing disparities in income and wealth distribution, fiscal policy strives to cultivate a more equitable socioeconomic landscape, wherein the fruits of economic progress are shared equitably across society.

Fiscal policy emerges as a multifaceted instrument wielded by governments to navigate the complexities of economic management. Through judicious manipulation of government spending, taxation and borrowing, policymakers seek to steer economies towards the shores of prosperity, stability, and equity. Yet, the efficacy of fiscal policy hinges upon adept policy formulation, diligent implementation, and adaptability to dynamic economic realities (Alberola *et al.,* 2021). In the intricate dance of economic governance, fiscal policy stands as a linchpin, shaping the contours of nations' economic destinies.

Fiscal Policy Instruments

Fiscal policy represents a critical component of governmental economic management, wielding considerable influence over the health and trajectory of economies. This section delves into the multifaceted mechanisms through which fiscal policy operates, encompassing government spending, taxation strategies and the intricacies of government borrowing.

Government Spending

Government spending serves as a pivotal tool for steering economic activity towards desired outcomes. Understanding the nuances between expansionary and contractionary spending illuminates the dynamic nature of fiscal policy.

a. **Expansionary vs. Contractionary Spending:** Expansionary spending entails deliberate increases in government outlays aimed at stimulating economic growth and bolstering demand during periods of recession or stagnation (as shown in Figure 1). Conversely, contractionary spending involves curbing expenditures to mitigate inflationary pressures or address budgetary constraints.

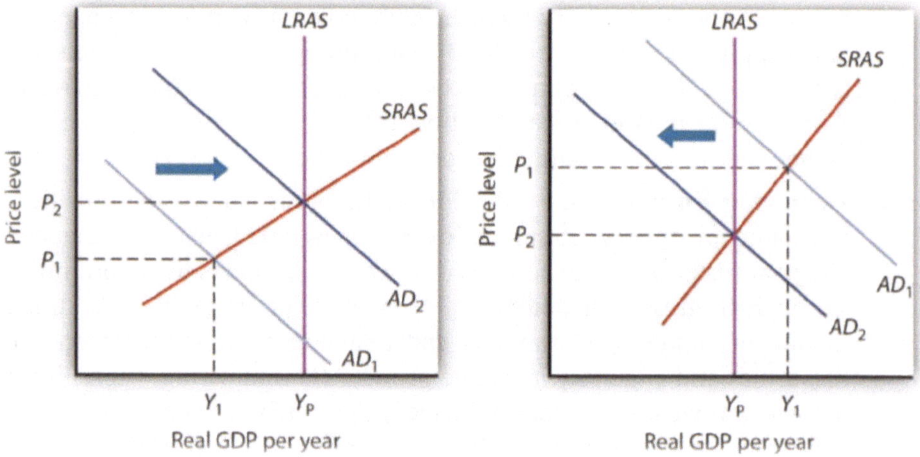

Fig. 1: Expansionary (in left) and Contractionary (in right) Spending

b. **Categories of Government Spending:** Government spending encompasses a broad spectrum of allocations, spanning crucial sectors such as infrastructure development, healthcare, education, defence, and social welfare programs. Strategic allocation within these categories can significantly impact long-term economic productivity and societal well-being.

Taxation

Taxation stands as a fundamental instrument for revenue generation and socio-economic engineering, characterized by its diverse forms and redistributive implications (as shown in Table 1).

a. **Direct vs. Indirect Taxes:** Direct taxes, levied directly on individuals or entities, include income taxes, corporate taxes and property taxes. In contrast, indirect taxes, such as value-added taxes (VAT) or sales taxes, are imposed on the purchase of goods and services, often shifting the burden across consumer bases.

b. **Progressive vs. Regressive Taxes:** Progressive taxation adopts a tiered approach, whereby tax rates escalate with income levels, aiming to redistribute wealth and alleviate income disparities. Conversely, regressive taxation exerts a disproportionate burden on lower-income segments, as the tax rate diminishes relative to income.

Table 1: Direct vs. Indirect vs. Progressive vs. Regressive Taxes

Feature	Direct Tax	Indirect Tax	Progressive Tax	Regressive Tax
Who Pays	Individual or Business directly to government	Consumer pays to business; government collects from business	Higher income earners pay a higher percentage	Lower income earners pay a higher percentage
Tax Base	Income, Profits, Wealth	Goods and Services	Income	Spending
Example	Income Tax, Corporate Tax	Sales Tax, VAT, Excise Duty	Federal Income Tax (US)	Sales Tax (most US states)
Impact	Can be progressive or proportional	Typically regressive	More equitable distribution of tax burden	Less equitable distribution of tax burden
Collection	More complex filing process	Easier to collect, often hidden	Varies depending on income brackets	Flat rate or decreases with income
Evasion	More possible	Less possible	Less likely for high earners	More likely for low earners

c. **Using Taxes to Influence Behaviour:** Governments leverage taxation as a mechanism to steer societal behaviour towards desired outcomes. Environmental taxes, for instance, incentivize eco-friendly practices while internalizing the externalities associated with pollution and resource depletion.

Government Borrowing

Government borrowing emerges as a critical strategy for financing deficits and catalysing investment, albeit with implications for intergenerational equity and fiscal sustainability.

a. **The Role of National Debt:** National debt reflects the cumulative borrowing undertaken by governments to finance budgetary shortfalls, infrastructure projects, or emergency expenditures. It serves as a barometer of fiscal health, albeit subject to nuanced interpretation concerning its sustainability and impact on future generations.

b. **Fiscal Sustainability:** Fiscal sustainability scrutinizes the long-term viability of government borrowing practices, weighing factors such as debt-to-GDP ratios, interest rate dynamics and demographic trends. Prudent fiscal management entails striking a delicate balance between stimulating economic growth & safeguarding against excessive debt accumulation, ensuring intergenerational equity and economic resilience.

Fiscal policy instruments wield profound influence over economic dynamics, underpinning governments' capacity to navigate challenges, foster growth and promote socio-economic well-being. A nuanced understanding of these mechanisms is indispensable for informed policymaking and effective stewardship of national economies (Devereux *et al.,* 2020).

Beyond Fiscal Measures

Financial markets are not only influenced by fiscal policies but also by a myriad of other factors that play a crucial role in shaping economic landscapes. Understanding these factors is imperative in comprehending the intricate workings of financial markets and their profound impact on economies. In this section, we delve into the significance of monetary policy, trade policy and regulatory policy, elucidating their nuances and implications.

Monetary Policy

Monetary policy, wielded primarily by central banks, constitutes a cornerstone of economic management. Through a delicate interplay of tools and strategies, central banks endeavour to regulate the money supply, interest rates and credit availability to achieve macroeconomic objectives.

a. **Role of Central Bank:** Central banks serve as the custodians of monetary policy, entrusted with the pivotal task of maintaining price stability and fostering sustainable economic growth. By meticulously monitoring key economic indicators such as inflation, unemployment and GDP growth, central banks formulate and execute monetary policies tailored to prevailing economic conditions.

b. **Interest Rates and Credit Availability:** One of the primary mechanisms through which central banks influence financial markets is the manipulation of interest rates. By adjusting benchmark interest rates, such as the federal funds rate in the United States, central banks seek to modulate borrowing costs, thereby stimulating or curbing consumer spending, investment and overall economic activity. Moreover, central banks also influence credit availability by employing tools like open market operations and reserve requirements to regulate the liquidity of commercial banks.

c. **Coordination with Fiscal Policy:** Effective coordination between monetary and fiscal policies is paramount for ensuring macroeconomic stability and efficacy. While fiscal policy pertains to government taxation and spending, monetary policy focuses on money supply and interest rates. Harmonizing these policies can amplify their collective impact on economic variables, promoting sustainable growth while mitigating inflationary pressures or recessionary risks.

Trade Policy

Trade policy plays a pivotal role in shaping the interconnected global economy, exerting a profound influence on financial markets, economic growth, and labour markets.

a. **Free Trade vs. Protectionism:** The perennial debate between free trade and protectionism underscores fundamental ideological differences regarding the optimal approach to international trade. Free trade advocates contend that removing barriers to trade fosters economic efficiency, enhances consumer welfare and promotes specialization (as shown in Table 2). Conversely, proponents of protectionism argue for safeguarding domestic industries through tariffs, quotas, and subsidies to shield them from foreign competition and preserve jobs.

Table 2: Free Trade vs. Protectionism

Feature	Free Trade	Protectionism
Prices	Generally lower	Can be higher to protect domestic industries
Consumer Choice	Wider variety of goods and services	May limit consumer choice
Jobs	May lead to job losses in some sectors	May protect jobs in certain industries
Economic Growth	Can lead to faster economic growth	May slow economic growth
Innovation	Can encourage innovation	May stifle innovation

b. **Impact on Economic Growth and Job Markets:** The ramifications of trade policy transcend national borders, reverberating across industries and labour markets. While free trade proponents assert that liberalizing trade spurs innovation, fosters competitiveness and fuels economic growth, critics caution against the potential adverse effects on domestic industries and employment. Trade agreements and tariffs can significantly impact job creation, wage levels and income distribution, underscoring the intricate interplay between trade policy and labour markets.

Regulatory Policy

Regulatory policy constitutes a critical framework governing the conduct of market participants, balancing the imperatives of market efficiency with safeguarding public interest and stability.

a. **Balancing Market Efficiency and Public Interest:** Regulatory frameworks seek to strike a delicate equilibrium between fostering vibrant, competitive markets and safeguarding consumers, investors, and systemic stability. Regulations span a broad spectrum, encompassing financial oversight, consumer protection, environmental stewardship and antitrust measures, among others. Effective regulatory policy aims to mitigate market failures, curb systemic risks and instil confidence in financial markets while facilitating innovation and entrepreneurship.

b. **Examples (Environmental Regulations, Antitrust Laws):** Exemplifying regulatory policy in action, environmental regulations mandate stringent standards and emissions controls to mitigate environmental degradation and promote sustainable development. Similarly, antitrust laws aim to curb monopolistic practices, promote market competition, and safeguard consumer welfare by preventing anti-competitive mergers and monopolistic behaviour.

   The efficacy of financial markets hinges not only on fiscal measures but also on a multifaceted interplay of monetary, trade and regulatory policies. Understanding and navigating these policy domains are essential for fostering robust, resilient economies and ensuring the continued vitality of financial markets as the lifeblood of global prosperity (Klimanov *et al.,* 2021).

Evaluating the Effectiveness of Economic Policies

Policymakers, armed with a myriad of tools and strategies, constantly endeavour to navigate the turbulent waters of economic fluctuations. However, the assessment of these policies is not a straightforward task; it requires a nuanced understanding of various economic indicators, coupled with an acute awareness of the challenges inherent in policy evaluation.

Measuring Economic Performance

a. **Gross Domestic Product (GDP):** At the heart of evaluating economic performance lies the Gross Domestic Product (GDP), a comprehensive measure of a nation's economic activity. GDP encapsulates the total value of all goods and services produced within a country's borders over a specified period. It serves as a barometer of economic health, reflecting the overall productivity and consumption patterns within an economy. Variations in GDP growth rates provide insights into the trajectory of economic expansion or contraction, guiding policymakers in fine-tuning their strategies accordingly.

b. **Unemployment Rate:** Another crucial metric in assessing economic performance is the unemployment rate. This metric delineates the proportion of the labour force that is actively seeking employment but remains jobless. A high unemployment rate signifies underutilization of human capital and potential inefficiencies within the labour market. Conversely, a declining unemployment rate suggests a burgeoning job market and greater economic vitality. Policymakers closely monitor fluctuations in unemployment rates to gauge the effectiveness of labour market policies and tailor interventions to alleviate unemployment woes.

c. **Inflation Rate:** Inflation, the persistent rise in the general price level of goods and services, is a critical parameter in economic evaluation. The inflation rate, typically measured through indices such as the Consumer Price Index (CPI), reflects the erosion of purchasing power over time. Moderate inflation is often deemed conducive to economic growth, as it incentivizes consumption and investment. However, runaway inflation can destabilize markets, erode consumer confidence, and impede long-term economic prosperity. Hence, policymakers meticulously monitor inflationary trends to calibrate monetary policies and maintain price stability (Almeida *et al.,* 2020).

Challenges of Policy Evaluation

a. **Time Lags:** One of the foremost challenges in evaluating economic policies is the presence of time lags. Economic policies, whether monetary or fiscal, often entail a gestation period before their full impact materializes. For instance, the effects of interest rate adjustments by central banks may not manifest immediately in consumer spending or investment decisions. Similarly, fiscal stimulus measures may take time to permeate through the economy and stimulate aggregate demand. As such, policymakers must exercise patience and foresight in interpreting the delayed repercussions of their policy interventions.

b. **Isolating the Impact of a Single Policy:** Isolating the impact of a single policy amidst the cacophony of external factors poses a formidable challenge in policy evaluation. Economic systems are intricate ecosystems where multiple variables interact in complex ways. Disentangling the effects of a specific policy from concurrent economic trends and external shocks necessitates sophisticated econometric techniques and rigorous empirical analysis. Moreover, policy synergies and spillover effects further blur the boundaries of causality, complicating the attribution of outcomes to individual policies.

The Importance of Transparency and Accountability

Transparency and accountability constitute the bedrock of effective policy evaluation. In democratic societies, policymakers are entrusted with the solemn responsibility of stewarding public resources and shaping the economic destiny of nations. Hence, transparency in policy formulation and implementation engenders public trust and fosters informed civic participation. Moreover, accountability mechanisms, encompassing periodic audits and performance evaluations, ensure that policymakers remain answerable to the electorate and adhere to the principles of good governance. By upholding transparency and accountability standards, policymakers bolster the legitimacy of their actions and fortify the social contract between the state and its citizens (Ando *et al.*, 2020).

Evaluating the effectiveness of economic policies demands a judicious synthesis of quantitative metrics, qualitative assessments, and contextual insights. By navigating the labyrinth of economic indicators and surmounting the challenges of policy evaluation, policymakers can chart a course towards sustainable growth, prosperity and equitable development.

Conclusion

Financial markets serve as the backbone of a healthy economy, channelling capital where it's most needed. A 2023 World Bank report highlights that economies with well-developed financial markets experience a significant boost in GDP per capita, averaging 1.8% higher compared to those with underdeveloped markets. This underscores the critical role financial markets play in facilitating business growth, innovation and ultimately, job creation. Efficient allocation of resources is another key function. By connecting investors with businesses and governments seeking capital, financial markets ensure funds flow towards productive endeavours. A 2022 McKinsey report estimates that the global private debt market reached a staggering $331 trillion in 2021, showcasing the immense capacity of financial markets to mobilize capital for large-scale projects and infrastructure development. However, it's crucial to acknowledge that financial markets are not without their vulnerabilities. The 2008 financial crisis serves as a stark reminder of the potential for instability and systemic risk. As we move forward, fostering robust regulatory frameworks and promoting responsible financial practices remain paramount in ensuring the continued health and stability of this vital economic lifeline.

References

Alberola, E., Arslan, Y., Cheng, G., & Moessner, R. (2021). Fiscal response to the COVID-19 crisis in advanced and emerging market economies. Pacific Economic Review, 26(4), 459-468.

Almeida, V., Barrios Cobos, S., Christl, M., De Poli, S., Tumino, A., & Van Der Wielen, W. (2020). Households' income and the cushioning effect of fiscal policy measures during the Great Lockdown (No. 06/2020). JRC Working Papers on Taxation and Structural Reforms.

Amores, A. F., Basso, H. S., Bischl, J. S., De Agostini, P., Poli, S. D., Dicarlo, E., ... & Riscado, S. (2023). Inflation, fiscal policy and inequality. ECB Occasional Paper, (2023/330).

Anderson, J., Bergamini, E., Brekelmans, S., Cameron, A., Darvas, Z., Jíménez, M. D., & Midões, C. (2020). The fiscal response to the economic fallout from the coronavirus. Bruegel datasets.

Ando, M., Furukawa, C., Nakata, D., & Sumiya, K. (2020). Fiscal responses to the COVID-19 crisis in Japan: the first six months. National Tax Journal, 73(3), 901-926.

Chugunov, I., Pasichnyi, M., Koroviy, V., Kaneva, T., & Nikitishin, A. (2021). Fiscal and monetary policy of economic development. European Journal of Sustainable Development, 10(1), 42-42.

Devereux, M. P., Güçeri, İ., Simmler, M., & Tam, E. H. (2020). Discretionary fiscal responses to the COVID-19 pandemic. Oxford Review of Economic Policy, 36(Supplement_1), S225-S241.

Karpova, V. V., Tischenko, V. F., Ostapenko, V. M., & Ivanov, Y. B. (2020). Anti-crisis fiscal measures in the European union during the COVID-19 pandemic and their impact on GDP.

Klimanov, V., Kazakova, S., Mikhaylova, A., & Safina, A. (2021). Fiscal resilience of Russia's regions in the face of COVID-19. Journal of Public Budgeting, Accounting & Financial Management, 33(1), 87-94.

Postula, M., & Radecka-Moroz, K. (2020). Fiscal policy instruments in environmental protection. Environmental impact assessment review, 84, 106435.

Romer, C. D. (2021). The fiscal policy response to the pandemic. Brookings Papers on Economic Activity, 89-110.

7

Public Finance Expenditure, Revenue and Debt Dynamics

Shweta Chaudhary and Ruch Rani Gangwar

Department of Agricultural Economics, Gobind Ballabh Pant University of Agriculture and Technology, Pantnagar, Uttarakhand

Abstract

Public finance plays a pivotal role in economic governance by managing government revenue, expenditures, and debt to ensure societal needs are met and economic stability is maintained. This chapter provides an overview of public finance, focusing on its significance, core components, functions, types, and causes, specifically emphasizing public revenue, expenditure, and debt. Public revenue, primarily sourced from taxes and non-tax revenues like fees and fines, fuels government operations, while public expenditure covers government spending on essential services and infrastructure, impacting production, distribution, consumption, and economic growth. Principles of public expenditure guide its allocation, emphasizing maximum social advantage, economy, sanction, and balanced budgets. Public debt arises when government spending surpasses revenue, leading to borrowing to cover deficits. It is classified based on duration, source, and purpose, with causes including war expenditures, budget deficits, and inefficiencies in public administration. Redemption of public debt is crucial to prevent government bankruptcy and instill confidence in lenders. Understanding public finance is vital for policymakers to make informed decisions regarding resource allocation and fiscal policy, promoting economic stability, societal well-being, and sustainable growth.

Keywords: *Public finance, revenue, expenditure, debt, taxation, government spending, fiscal policy, economic stability.*

Introduction

The field of public finance is a critical aspect of economic governance that delves into how governments manage their revenue, expenditures, and debt to fulfill societal needs and ensure economic stability. Public finance encompasses the financial activities of governments at various levels, including national, state, and local, focusing on the income and expenditure of public authorities and the underlying principles guiding these financial transactions.

Significance of Public Finance

- **Role in Society:** Public finance is a branch of public policy and economics concerned with how governments raise funds, allocate resources, and address economic and social needs.
- **Government Functions:** Governments provide public goods and services like infrastructure, defense, education, and social welfare programs that are essential for societal well-being.
- **Market Correction:** Public finance enables governments to address market failures by providing public goods that individuals or businesses would not produce efficiently on their own.
- **Income Redistribution:** Through programs like social security and welfare, public finance helps moderate income disparities by supporting those in need.

Core Components of Public Finance

Public finance encompasses the management of a country's revenue, expenditures, and debt load through various government and quasi-government institutions. The essential components of public finance include tax collection, budgeting, expenditures, deficit/surplus, and national debt.

1. **Tax Collection:** Tax collection stands as the primary revenue source for governments, encompassing various taxes like sales tax, income tax, estate tax, and property tax. Additionally, revenue from duties, tariffs on imports, and public services contribute to the government's income stream.
2. **Budgeting:** Budgeting is a crucial aspect of public finance, representing a plan outlining the government's intended expenditures for a fiscal year. In the U.S., for instance, the president submits a budget request to Congress, which then crafts bills for specific budget aspects, culminating in the president signing them into law. Budgeting ensures a balance between revenue generation and planned expenses.
3. **Expenditures:** Government expenditures cover all the money spent on activities and programs to support society, including social programs, education, and infrastructure. Much of government spending focuses on income or wealth redistribution to benefit society. The actual expenditures may exceed or fall short of the budget, leading to deficits or surpluses.

4. **Deficit/Surplus:** A deficit occurs when government spending surpasses revenue, necessitating borrowing and national debt issuance to cover the shortfall. Conversely, a surplus arises when expenditures are lower than revenue collected. In the case of a deficit, the government funds the difference by borrowing money and issuing national debt, managed by entities like the U.S. Treasury and the Office of Debt Management.
5. **National Debt:** During deficit years, governments issue national debt to bridge the gap between expenditures and revenue. The U.S. Treasury is responsible for issuing debt, while the Office of Debt Management decides on selling government securities to investors. National debt plays a crucial role in financing deficits and managing the financial health of governments.

Function of Public Finance

Public finance serves several crucial functions that are essential for the economic well-being and development of a nation. Based on the provided sources, here are the key functions of public finance:

1. **Managing Public Revenue and Expenditure:** Public finance ensures the proper utilization of resources by managing government revenue and expenditure effectively. This function involves allocating funds to various sectors like education, healthcare, infrastructure, and defense to meet societal needs and promote economic growth.
2. **Establishing Price Stability and Reducing Inflation:** Public finance plays a role in maintaining price stability and reducing inflation within the economy. By implementing sound fiscal policies, governments can help stabilize prices and control inflationary pressures, contributing to economic stability.
3. **Providing Necessary Infrastructure:** Public finance is instrumental in funding the development of essential infrastructure such as roads, bridges, schools, and hospitals. Investing in infrastructure is vital for economic growth, job creation, and improving the overall quality of life for citizens.
4. **Promoting Overall Economic Development:** Public finance supports public development initiatives that lead to the overall development of the economy. By investing in key sectors and projects, governments can stimulate economic growth, attract investments, and create opportunities for businesses and individuals.
5. **Maintaining Transparency in Public Policies:** Public finance ensures transparency in public policies and the management of public revenue and

expenditure. Transparency is crucial for building trust, accountability, and ensuring that public funds are used efficiently and effectively for the benefit of society.

6. **Budget Comparison and Policy Modification:** Public finance involves comparing the current financial position with public budgets and making necessary policy adjustments to manage the economy effectively. This function helps governments align their financial policies with economic goals and changing circumstances.
7. **Monitoring Policy Effectiveness:** Public finance monitors the effectiveness of different financial policies to assess their impact on the economy. By evaluating the outcomes of fiscal measures, governments can refine their policies to achieve desired economic objectives and address emerging challenges.
8. **Preparing Economic Policies for Growth:** Public finance plays a crucial role in preparing economic policies that drive the nation's growth and development. By formulating strategic financial plans, governments can create an environment conducive to economic prosperity, innovation, and sustainable development.

Types of Public Finance

The **public finance theory** comprises of a series of inflows and outflows that comprise to become the body of work it turns out to be for the government and its citizens. Let us understand its types through the explanation below.

A. Public Revenue

B. Public Expenditure

C. Public Debt

A. Public Revenue: The Income received by the different sources is known as public revenue. It includes taxation policies, fees, fines, etc.

Sources of Public Revenue

Two sources of public revenue are:

1. Tax revenue
2. Non- tax revenue

1. Tax Revenue: The chief source of public revenue is tax. To define, tax is said to be compulsory payment made to the government without expecting any direct benefit. It is classified in two types.

i) **Direct taxes-** Progressive in nature, burden can't be imposed on another person.

Example- Income tax, expenditure tax, etc.

ii) Indirect taxes– It cannot be shift to another person, regressive in nature.

Example- Sales tax, GST, excise duty, custom duty, etc.

2. Nontax revenue: It comprises all revenues apart from taxes accumulated to the government. These revenues are funds that are generated from internal source[8].

i. Interest receipts on loans
ii. Revenue from government activities like railway
iii. Receipts of currency notes, mint, etc.

Importance source of Non-Tax Revenue

1. Fees: Fees are charged and become payable whenever you avail any service rendered by the government. This includes education fees, fees paid to get certain certificates and licenses, property registration fees, business registration fees, etc.
2. Fines and Penalties: Fines and penalties are assessed against people who violate the country's laws and regulations. For example, tax evasion carries heavy consequences from the government. Violations of environmental or corporate governance regulations are punishable by both penalties and imprisonment. At a basic level, you must pay a fee if you run a red light or violate a traffic rule. It is important to note that the purpose of fines and penalties is not to produce government money, but to impose law and order in the country by penalizing those who do not comply.
3. Gifts, Grants and Donations: The government frequently receives gifts and donations from inhabitants of the country, which serve as one source of governmental money. The government may also receive donations from other countries' governments or agencies established to assist countries, such as the United Nations. However, these types of government revenue sources are not recurrent and cannot be completely relied upon.
4. Special Evaluation: The payment made by property owners in a specific locality in exchange for government-provided special facilities is referred to as special evaluation or assessment. For instance, governing bodies may assess a fee for the provision of an underground drainage pipe system to a gated community or the water delivery to the area.

5. Public Companies Surplus: A considerable number of public corporations that provide services to the populace are owned and managed by the government. Referred to as economic income, the profits they generate are among the most significant sources of revenue for the Indian government. ONGC, Power Finance Corporation, and the State Bank of India are examples of public corporations.
6. Forfeitures: This constitutes a relatively insignificant portion of the government's non-tax revenue in India. Revenue is generated through the forfeiture of assets or security deposits. Non-performance of a contract by any of the parties who entered it is also grounds for forfeiture.
7. Funds Borrowed: International organizations such as the International Monetary Fund and the World Bank are among the foreign nations, citizens, and institutions from which the government may borrow funds. This assists in meeting the government's expenditures.
8. Liquor Charges: Liquor serves as a substantial revenue generator for both the federal and state governments. This is because states impose excise tax on both the production and sale of alcoholic beverages. Additionally, some states, including Tamil Nadu, tax alcohol with VAT. Additional levies imposed by states encompass transportation fees, special tariffs on imported foreign liquor, and registration charges for the brand and label.

B. Public Expenditure: Public expenditure refers to the expenses which the Government incurs for its own maintenance as also for society and the economy.

Public expenditure can be defined as, "The expenditure incurred by public authorities like central and local governments to satisfy the collective social wants of the people is known as public expenditure."

In developing countries, public expenditure policy not only accelerates economic growth & promotes employment opportunities but also plays a useful role in reducing poverty and inequalities in income distribution.

Effect of Public Expenditure

1. **Effects on Production-** Public expenditure impacts production by influencing the ability and willingness of individuals to work, save, and invest. Investments in education, healthcare, and infrastructure can enhance workforce efficiency and productivity. It also affects the allocation of resources among different industries and trade, shaping the pattern of production.

2. **Effects on Distribution-** Public expenditure plays a crucial role in promoting equitable distribution of income and wealth. Programs like poor relief and old-aged allowances benefit the less affluent more significantly than the wealthy, contributing to social welfare and reducing income disparities.
3. **Effects on Consumption-** Public expenditure can influence consumption patterns by providing social security, enhancing purchasing power, and fostering confidence among the populace. Investments in public services like education and healthcare can lead to increased consumer spending.
4. **Effects on Economic Growth-** Public expenditure impacts economic growth by stimulating the will and capacity of individuals to work, save, and invest. It can enhance efficiency, productivity, and overall economic performance. Investments in infrastructure, education, and healthcare can contribute to sustained economic growth.
5. **Effects on Economic Stability-** Public expenditure can contribute to economic stability by providing a framework for sustainable growth and development. By investing in key sectors and promoting social welfare, public expenditure can help maintain a stable economic environment.

Principles or Canons of Public Expenditure

1. **The Principle of Maximum Social Advantage** - This principle emphasizes that all public expenditure should aim to achieve maximum social benefit. The focus is on promoting general welfare and benefiting society rather than specific groups or individuals.
2. **The Principle of Economy-** The principle of economy stresses the importance of avoiding extravagance and waste in public spending. It highlights the need to prevent duplication of expenditure and overlapping authorities to ensure efficient use of resources
3. **The Principle of Sanction** - According to this principle, public expenditure should be sanctioned by competent authorities before being incurred. Proper authorization is essential to prevent extravagance and ensure that funds are spent on approved purposes.
4. **The Principle of Balanced Budgets** - The principle of balanced budgets suggests that governments should strive for financial equilibrium, where expenditures do not exceed revenues. Maintaining a balance between income and expenditure is crucial for fiscal stability and sustainability.

Causes of Increase in Public Expenditure

1. Population and land area expansion
2. Development of state operations
3. Increased cost and price level of public services
4. Accumulation of national resources
5. Tax capacity, as an example, a low-income versus high-income economy.
6. Conflict and conflict prevention
7. Provision of public utility services, including an expanding array of such services as transportation, water, and electricity.
8. Efficient product mix, in the sense that an increase in GNP signifies a shift from an agricultural to an industrial economy, resulting in a rise in public expenditure and commodities for society.
9. Granting more funds for social services, including healthcare, public health initiatives, and education.
10. Technological innovations and changes necessitate expanded or novel production methods within the public sector.
11. The expansion of the public sector can be attributed to the influence of socialistic tendencies in the contemporary era.
12. Defective financial and civil administration is prevalent, as evidenced by the duplication and superfluous expansion of government agencies. If so, the number of resources allocated and wasted is not insignificant.
13. Social and political factors
14. After the thirties, there was an increase in welfare activities and the growth of transfer expenditures, such as free medical assistance and free education.
15. Stipulation of complete employment, which means that all individuals must be employed.
16. Economic development, including social and economic costs.

D. Public Debt

Public debt refers to loans incurred by the government to finance its activities when current revenue falls short of public expenditures. It is borrowed internally or externally from various sources like banks, individuals, or international institutions. Public debt is classified into internal and external debt, short-term and long-term loans, funded and unfunded debt, voluntary and compulsory loans, and redeemable and irredeemable debt. Productive debt is used for income-generating purposes, enhancing the country's productive capacity, while unproductive debt, like loans for war or relief work, does not contribute to economic growth. Methods of redeeming public debt include refunding, issuing new bonds to pay off matured loans, and conversion, reducing interest burdens by converting high-interest loans to low-interest ones.

Classification of Public Debt

1. **Internal and External Debt:** Internal debt refers to loans floated within the country, while external debt is borrowed from foreign entities[12].
2. **Short-term and Long-term Debt:** Short-term loans have a maturity period of less than 90 days, while long-term loans have a tenure exceeding 10 years.
3. **Funded and Unfunded Debt:** Funded debt is long-term and marketable, requiring a separate fund for repayment, while unfunded debt is short-term and lacks a separate repayment fund.
4. **Redeemable and Irredeemable Debt:** Redeemable debt is repayable on a future date, while irredeemable debt only pays interest regularly without a promise to repay the principal.
5. **Productive and Unproductive Debt:** Productive debt is used for income-generating activities, enhancing the economy's production capacity, while unproductive debt does not create assets or income.

Causes of Public Debt

1. War or war-preparedness, including nuclear programs
2. To cover the budget deficits on current account
3. To undertake public welfare schemes
4. Urge for economic growth
5. Inefficiencies of public organizations and corruption

Redemption of Public Debt

- Redemption of debt pertains to the repayment of a public loan; while it is obligatory for public debt to be repaid, it is also a desirable outcome.
- Periodically, the government is obligated to redeem its debt to bolster lender confidence and avert bankruptcy.

Conclusion

It can be concluded that public finance serves as the backbone of economic governance, pivotal in maintaining societal welfare and economic stability.

By effectively managing revenue, expenditures, and debt, governments can meet societal needs, stimulate economic growth, and ensure fiscal sustainability. The core components of public finance, encompassing tax collection, budgeting, expenditures, deficit/surplus management, and national debt, lay the groundwork for efficient resource allocation and fiscal discipline. Through its various functions, including establishing price stability, promoting infrastructure development, and preparing growth-oriented economic policies, public finance plays a vital role in shaping the economic and social landscape. Understanding the types and causes of public finance, such as revenue, expenditure, and debt, provides crucial insights into the challenges and opportunities governments face in fiscal management, from funding public services to addressing budget deficits and managing debt levels. Public finance is instrumental in fostering sustainable growth and development, ensuring that resources are allocated efficiently to maximize societal welfare and long-term prosperity.

References

Anonymous, 2013. Public Finance: Meaning, Definition, Scope, and Functions. Greek for Greek.

https://corporatefinanceinstitute.com/resources/economics/public-finance/

https://en.wikipedia.org/wiki/Public_finance

https://www.careerservicestation.com/a-brief-introduction-to-public-finance/

https://www.nagwa.com/en/explainers/743168592465/

https://navi.com/blog/public-finance/

https://www.geeksforgeeks.org/canons-of-public-expenditure/

The Economic times, 2024. Retrieved from https://economictimes.indiatimes.com/definition/non-tax-revenue.

https://www.wallstreetmojo.com/public-finance/

https://www.economicsdiscussion.net/economy/11-main-principles-of-public-expenditure-discussed/1938

https://homework.study.com/explanation/these-are-principles-proposed-to-govern-public-expenditure-decisions-they-are-also-referred-to-as-the-canons-of-public-expenditure-which-are-they.html

https://unstats.un.org/unsd/statcom/13th-session/documents/doc65/1965-325-PublicDebt-E.pdf

https://www.gacbe.ac.in/pdf/ematerial/18MEC32C-U4.pdf

https://www.economicsdiscussion.net/debt-2/public-debt-meaning-classification-and- method-of-redemption/17472.

8

Banking on Growth The Role of Finance in Development

Km Deepshikha, Monmath Gopal and Sachin Kumar Verma

Acharya Narendra Deva University of Agriculture and Technology Kumarganj Ayodhya, Uttar Pradesh

Abstract

This abstract provides a comprehensive overview of key topics related to financial inclusion, banking regulation, sustainable development financing, and the transformative potential of digital payments and blockchain technology. It begins by highlighting the fundamental importance of access to banking services for underserved populations, emphasizing the role of savings accounts, credit facilities, and payment systems in empowering individuals and catalysing economic development. Microfinance emerges as a critical tool for small business development, particularly in marginalized communities, while financial inclusion is shown to have significant impacts on poverty alleviation and social inclusion. The abstract then delves into the role of banking regulation in maintaining financial stability, outlining challenges such as regulatory complexity and the need to balance stability with innovation. Strategies for enhancing financial stability are proposed, including robust regulatory frameworks and effective risk management practices. In the context of sustainable development financing, various mechanisms are explored, including mobilizing domestic resources, private sector engagement, and innovative financing instruments. The abstract also underscores the importance of international cooperation and partnerships in achieving the Sustainable Development Goals (SDGs). Lastly, the transformative potential of digital payments and blockchain technology is discussed, highlighting their role in fostering financial inclusion, promoting economic empowerment, and supporting sustainable development initiatives, particularly in underserved regions. In essence, this abstract provides a comprehensive overview of key concepts and strategies aimed at fostering economic growth and sustainable development on a global scale.

Keywords: *Finances, Banking regulation, financial inclusion, SDGs, Financial stability, Banking Services, Microfinance.*

Introduction

The backbone of economic growth are financial systems, which act as the channels for managing risks, facilitating investments, and allocating resources within an economy. Financial systems, which consist of a wide range of organizations, markets, and tools, are essential for coordinating the movement of capital between surplus (savers) and deficit (borrowers) units. They basically provide risk management, resource allocation, payment facilitation, and intermediation, among other crucial responsibilities. This complex network of interconnected roles makes sure that money is effectively allocated to its most profitable uses and offers safeguards against risk and smooth transactions. It supports sustainable growth and development by acting as the lifeblood of the economy.

A wide range of elements, such as macroeconomic conditions, regulatory frameworks, and technological breakthroughs, influence the evolution and dynamics of financial systems. Financial systems have changed significantly over time because of new difficulties and shifting environments. Resilience, creativity, and adaptation have been characteristics of the growth of finance, from the rise of modern banking institutions to the introduction of modern financial technology solutions. It is essential to solving urgent global issues including climate change, inequality, and sustainable development in addition to fostering economic growth and societal improvement. Financial institutions and stakeholders are using their resources to leverage sustainable finance practices, impact investment, and green finance efforts to create positive social and environmental consequences. It can be a strong tool for bringing about positive change and creating a more sustainable and equitable future.

History

Early financial systems emerged in ancient civilizations, reflecting the economic needs and structures of early societies. In Mesopotamia, Egypt, and ancient China, rudimentary forms of financial transactions facilitated trade through barter and credit arrangements. Temples and religious institutions served as early banks, offering safekeeping services, and extending credit to merchants and individuals. In medieval Europe and Asia, formalized banking practices began to emerge, with merchant guilds and wealthy families establishing early banking institutions to support trade and commerce. These early financial systems laid the groundwork for the development of sophisticated financial institutions and practices, shaping the trajectory of finance throughout history. After that industrial revolution signifying a shift from agrarian economies to industrialized ones. This transition brought about a surge in demand for capital to fuel large-scale industrial projects. Consequently, modern banking systems, stock markets, and financial intermediaries emerged to meet this demand, mobilizing savings, and facilitating investment in industrial ventures. These institutions played a pivotal role in channelling funds towards productive uses, supporting industrial growth, and driving economic development.

The 19th and 20th centuries marked a period of rapid globalization in finance, propelled by advancements in technology and shifts in geopolitical dynamics. This globalization revolutionized financial systems, leading to the expansion of global financial markets and institutions. It facilitated the seamless flow of capital across borders, enabling investments and transactions on an international scale. Moreover, this era witnessed significant innovations in financial instruments and risk management practices, aimed at managing the complexities of cross-border transactions and enhancing financial stability.

Despite growth spurts, financial systems have faced recurring instability and crises. Historical crises like the Great Depression, Asian financial crisis, and the 2008 global financial crisis exposed systemic vulnerabilities, prompting urgent reforms. In response, regulatory actions were taken with the goal of improving fiscal resilience, risk management, and oversight. These crises operate as ominous reminders of the necessity of proactive safeguards and close observation to prevent future shocks and maintain the integrity and stability of financial systems in the face of shifting economic conditions. particularly in the latter half of the 20th century, have revolutionized financial systems. The computerization of financial processes and the advent of the internet paved the way for electronic banking, online trading platforms, and the emergence of digital currencies. These innovations have democratized access to finance and enhanced efficiency and transparency in financial markets.

Importance

- One of the primary functions of financial institutions is to mobilize savings from households, businesses, and other entities. Financial institutions stimulate economic growth by pooling these funds and using them for profitable ventures like corporate expansions, infrastructural initiatives, and technological advancements.
- Financial institutions provide a wide range of financial goods and services that allow people and companies to disperse risk and improve financial stability by diversifying their investment portfolios. The diversification of risks has a crucial role in protecting against market fluctuations, economic downturns, and unexpected incidents, ultimately promoting a stable financial ecosystem.

- Financial institutions facilitate access to credit, enabling individuals and businesses to pursue various endeavours. Whether funding education, housing, infrastructure projects, or entrepreneurial ventures, access to credit empowers individuals and businesses to invest in their futures and contribute to economic development.
- Financial institutions have a major impact on economic growth because they offer opportunities for investment and entrepreneurship. Their assistance to small and large firms promotes innovation, the creation of jobs, and the generation of income, which helps to reduce poverty and improve society.
- Many financial institutions are committed to promoting financial inclusion by extending their services to underserved and marginalized populations. By reaching out to these segments of society, financial institutions empower individuals with access to savings, credit, insurance, and other financial services.

Financial Inclusion and Economic Empowerment

Financial inclusion serves as a cornerstone for economic empowerment, ensuring that individuals and communities have access to essential banking services and resources. This chapter delves into three key aspects:

- **Access to Banking Services:** Access to banking services is fundamental for the economic empowerment of underserved populations. Basic financial services such as savings accounts, credit facilities, and payment systems play a pivotal role in enabling individuals to manage their finances efficiently and engage in economic endeavours. Savings accounts provide a secure means of accumulating funds, allowing individuals to plan, build assets, and withstand financial shocks. Access to credit facilities empowers entrepreneurs and small businesses to invest in their ventures, expand operations, and seize opportunities for growth. Moreover, payment systems facilitate transactions, enabling individuals to participate more actively in economic activities, whether through purchasing goods and services or conducting business transactions. Overall, providing banking services to underserved populations not only fosters financial inclusion but also catalyses economic development by unlocking the potential of individuals to participate more fully in the economy.
- **Microfinance and Small Business Development:** Microfinance plays a crucial role in fostering small business development by providing financial services to entrepreneurs who lack the ability to use

conventional banking. Small loans, savings accounts, and other financial products catered to the requirements of marginalized groups and other underprivileged populations are provided by microfinance organizations. Microfinance enables people to start or grow their enterprises by giving them access to capital and financial resources, which promotes economic growth and job prospects. These small enterprises support the community's economy by creating jobs, boosting demand locally, and encouraging entrepreneurship. Additionally, microfinance programs frequently give women and other vulnerable groups priority, advancing social inclusion and gender equality. In general, microfinance acts as a catalyst for sustainable development, empowering people to break the cycle of poverty and enhance their quality of life through small company development and entrepreneurship.

- **Impacts of Financial Inclusion on Poverty Alleviation:** Financial inclusion gives people the ability to handle their money more skilfully by giving them access to necessary financial services including insurance, credit facilities, and savings accounts. They can accumulate assets, manage their spending in hard times, and make investments in vital sectors like healthcare and education. Financial access barriers can be removed to help people take advantage of economic opportunities, increase their productivity, and raise their standard of living. Furthermore, to address underlying disparities and advance social inclusion, financial inclusion projects frequently focus on women and underrepresented communities. Through promoting long-term economic stability and prosperity, empirical data indicates that greater financial inclusion is associated with lower rates of poverty and helps to accomplish sustainable development goals.

Role of Banking Regulation in Financial Stability

Banking regulations function as crucial safeguards for maintaining the stability of financial systems. Crafted to counter inherent risks within financial landscapes, these regulations serve to temper excessive speculation and shield the interests of depositors and investors alike. Through mechanisms such as capital requirements, liquidity standards, and risk management guidelines, regulations compel banks to operate with prudence and uphold robust financial positions resilient to economic fluctuations. Capital requirements mandate that banks maintain adequate reserves relative to their assets, thereby serving as a protective buffer against potential losses. Liquidity standards ensure that banks uphold liquid assets to meet their obligations promptly, reinforcing their ability to navigate periods of financial strain. Furthermore, risk management guidelines cultivate a climate of prudent risk assessment and mitigation strategies within banks, fostering resilience against unforeseen challenges. Deposit insurance schemes by assuring depositors of reimbursement in the event of bank insolvencies, thereby instilling confidence in the banking system, and mitigating the risk of bank runs. Altogether, banking regulations play an indispensable role in fostering financial stability by promoting responsible banking practices and bolstering trust and resilience in the financial sector.

Challenges in Banking Regulations

- **Complexity of Financial Markets:** The intricate nature of financial markets and products poses a significant challenge for regulators. Rapid advancements and innovations often outpace regulatory frameworks, making it difficult for regulators to effectively anticipate and address emerging risks.
- **Regulatory Arbitrage:** Institutions may exploit regulatory loopholes or engage in cross-border activities to evade oversight, leading to regulatory arbitrage. This practice undermines the effectiveness of regulations and creates regulatory blind spots, increasing systemic risks within the banking sector.
- **Balancing Stability and Innovation:** Regulators face the delicate task of balancing the need for financial stability with promoting innovation and competitiveness in the banking sector. Overly restrictive regulations may stifle innovation and impede economic growth, while lax regulations can lead to excessive risk-taking and instability.
- **Compliance Burden:** Compliance with banking regulations imposes significant costs and administrative burdens on financial institutions. Meeting regulatory requirements often necessitates substantial investments in compliance infrastructure, which can strain resources and hinder operational efficiency.
- **Globalization and Cross-Border Issues:** The globalization of financial markets complicates banking regulation, as institutions operate across multiple jurisdictions with varying regulatory frameworks. Harmonizing regulations and addressing cross-border challenges require international cooperation and coordination among regulators.
- **Evolving Technological Landscape:** Rapid technological advancements, such as fintech innovations and digitalization, present new challenges for banking regulation. Regulators must adapt to

technological changes and address cybersecurity risks, data privacy concerns, and the emergence of new digital banking models to ensure the integrity and stability of the banking sector in the digital age.

Strategies for Enhancing Financial Stability

- **Robust Regulatory Frameworks:** Implement comprehensive regulations that cover all aspects of financial activities, including banking, securities, and insurance, to mitigate risks and ensure compliance with international standards.
- **Effective Supervision and Oversight:** Strengthen supervisory mechanisms to monitor financial institutions and markets, ensuring they operate prudently and manage risks appropriately. This oversight should include regular inspections, stress tests, and enforcement actions when necessary.
- **Risk Management Practices:** Encourage financial institutions to adopt robust risk management practices, including proper assessment, measurement, and mitigation of various risks such as credit, market, liquidity, and operational risks.
- **Capital Adequacy Requirements:** Set minimum capital requirements for financial institutions to ensure they have sufficient buffers to absorb losses during adverse economic conditions. This helps enhance the resilience of the financial system.
- **Liquidity Management:** Implement liquidity regulations and standards to guarantee that financial institutions maintain enough liquidity to fulfil their responsibilities, particularly in times of market stress or abrupt withdrawals.
- **Resolution Mechanisms:** Establish effective resolution frameworks to address the failure of financial institutions in an orderly manner, minimizing systemic disruptions and protecting depositors and creditors.
- **Enhanced Transparency and Disclosure:** Promote transparency and disclosure requirements for financial institutions to provide stakeholders with accurate and timely information about their financial condition, risks, and performance.
- **Financial Education and Consumer Protection:** Invest in financial literacy programs to empower consumers with knowledge about financial products and services, enabling them to make informed decisions. Additionally, enforce regulations to protect consumers from abusive practices and ensure fair treatment.

- **International Cooperation & Coordination:** Strengthen collaboration with international counterparts to address cross-border financial risks, harmonize regulatory standards, and facilitate information sharing and crisis management.
- **Contingency Planning and Crisis Preparedness:** Develop contingency plans and crisis management frameworks to anticipate and respond to potential systemic risks or financial crises, including coordination with central banks, regulatory agencies, and government authorities.

Financing Sustainable Development Goals (SDGs)

- **Mobilizing Domestic Resources:** Encourage domestic resource mobilization through taxation, efficient public expenditure management, and improved governance to fund SDG-related initiatives. This includes broadening the tax base, combatting tax evasion, and ensuring fair and transparent tax systems.
- **Private Sector Engagement:** Facilitate private sector investment in sustainable development projects by creating an enabling environment through policies that incentivize responsible business practices, promote public-private partnerships (PPPs), and reduce investment risks.
- **Impact Investing:** Promote impact investing, which involves investing in companies, organizations, and projects with the intention of generating positive social and environmental impact alongside financial returns. This can attract capital towards SDG-aligned initiatives while addressing pressing societal challenges.
- **Development Finance Institutions (DFIs):** Strengthen DFIs and multilateral development banks (MDBs) to provide long-term financing for SDG projects in developing countries. DFIs can leverage their resources to mobilize additional private sector investment and support innovative financing mechanisms.
- **Innovative Financing Mechanisms:** Explore and develop innovative financing mechanisms such as green bonds, social impact bonds, and results-based financing to attract new sources of capital for SDG implementation. These mechanisms can help bridge financing gaps and align investor interests with sustainable development objectives.
- **Official Development Assistance (ODA):** Maintain and increase ODA commitments from developed countries to support SDG implementation in low-income and least developed countries, particularly in sectors such as health, education, and infrastructure where public investment is crucial.

- **Debt Relief and Financial Instruments:** Provide debt relief and restructuring for highly indebted countries to free up resources for investment in sustainable development priorities. Additionally, explore financial instruments such as debt-for-nature swaps and climate resilience bonds to address both financial and environmental challenges.
- **International Cooperation and Partnerships:** Foster international cooperation and partnerships among governments, international organizations, civil society, and the private sector to pool resources, share knowledge, and coordinate efforts towards achieving the SDGs. This includes leveraging global initiatives like the UN Sustainable Development Goals Fund and the Global Partnership for Sustainable Development Data.
- **Capacity Building and Technical Assistance:** Support capacity building and provide technical assistance to developing countries to strengthen their financial management systems, improve project planning and implementation, and enhance their ability to attract and effectively utilize development finance for SDG achievement.
- **Measurement and Monitoring:** Develop robust monitoring and evaluation frameworks to track progress towards SDG financing targets, assess the impact of investments, and ensure accountability and transparency in the use of resources allocated for sustainable development purposes.

Digital Payments and Financial Inclusion

Digital payments are a game-changer for financial inclusion, especially in areas with limited access to traditional banking services. People can use their mobile phones or other digital devices to easily conduct financial transactions by utilizing digital wallets and mobile money systems. This technological innovation significantly reduces reliance on physical currency, streamlines transaction processes and lowers associated costs, thus facilitating greater accessibility to financial services for those previously excluded from the formal banking sector. Moreover, the widespread adoption of digital payments by governments and financial institutions has profound implications for socioeconomic development. Policymakers and other stakeholders can successfully close the gap between underserved populations and formal financial networks by giving priority to the development of digital payment infrastructure. In addition to encouraging economic empowerment at the individual and household levels, this strategic focus on digital financial inclusion also stimulates larger economic growth and poverty reduction initiatives. Additionally, by promoting resilience and improving financial stability within communities, the shift to digital payments supports sustainable development. Digital payments boost the foundation of sustainable development projects by making it easier for individuals to obtain financial services and enabling small businesses to engage more actively in the economy.

Blockchain and Cryptocurrencies in Development Finance

Blockchain technology and cryptocurrencies have the potential to transform development finance by providing secure, transparent, and decentralized solutions for financial transactions and asset management. Blockchain is a distributed ledger technology that enables peer-to-peer transactions without the need for intermediaries, offering enhanced security, immutability, and efficiency. Cryptocurrencies, such as Bitcoin and Ethereum, are digital assets that operate on blockchain networks and can be used for cross-border remittances, fundraising through initial coin offerings (ICOs), and decentralized finance (DeFi) applications. In the context of development finance, blockchain and cryptocurrencies can facilitate transparent and accountable aid distribution, streamline remittance payments, improve land and property rights management, and enable access to capital for underserved populations.

Conclusion

Financial inclusion serves as a bedrock for economic empowerment, providing marginalized communities with access to vital banking services, fostering entrepreneurship and enabling individuals to participate more actively in the economy. Microfinance initiatives have proven instrumental in bolstering small business development and lifting individuals out of poverty, while also promoting gender equality and social inclusion. However, navigating the complexities of regulatory frameworks amidst evolving financial landscapes presents significant challenges, underscoring the need for ongoing adaptation and international cooperation. In financing the Sustainable Development Goals (SDGs), a diverse array of strategies must be employed, ranging from mobilizing domestic resources and engaging the private sector to exploring innovative financing mechanisms and enhancing international partnerships. These efforts are essential for addressing global challenges, advancing social progress, and building resilient, inclusive societies. Furthermore, the transformative potential of digital payments and blockchain technology cannot be overstated. By expanding access to financial services, reducing transaction costs and enhancing transparency, these technologies hold promise in advancing financial inclusion, empowering communities and accelerating progress towards the SDGs.

To successfully traverse the intricacies of global finance, our strategy must continue to be based on collaboration, creativity and diversity. Through the adoption of these principles and the utilization of the combined knowledge and assets of various stakeholders, we may guide the course towards a future that is sustainable, fair, and successful for everybody.

References

Awrey, D. (2012). Complexity, innovation, and the regulation of modern financial markets. Harv. Bus. L. Rev., 2, 235.

Barua, S. (2020). Financing sustainable development goals: A review of challenges and mitigation strategies. Business Strategy & Development, 3(3), 277-293.

Basdekis, C., Christopoulos, A., Katsampoxakis, I. et al. FinTech's rapid growth and its effect on the banking sector. J Bank Financ Technol 6, 159–176 (2022).

Battilossi, S., Yago, K. (2020). Introduction: New Research in Monetary History – A Map. In: Battilossi, S., Cassis, Y., Yago, K. (eds) Handbook of the History of Money and Currency. Springer, Singapore.

H.R.Machiraju, Merchant banking, third Edition, New age international publishers.

https://www.graygroupintl.com/blog/financial-inclusion

Javaid, M., Haleem, A., Singh, R. P., Suman, R., & Khan, S. (2022). A review of Blockchain Technology applications for financial services. BenchCouncil Transactions on Benchmarks, Standards and Evaluations, 2(3), 100073.

Kose, M. A., & Ohnsorge, F. (Eds.). (2021). A decade after the global recession: Lessons and challenges for emerging and developing economies. World Bank Publications.

Saha, S. K., & Qin, J. (2023). Financial inclusion and poverty alleviation: an empirical examination. Economic Change and Restructuring, 56(1), 409-440.

Schinasi, G. J. 8 Challenges Posed by the Globalization of Finance and Risk. In Safeguarding Financial Stability. International Monetary Fund.

Xi, W., & Wang, Y. (2023). Digital financial inclusion and quality of economic growth. Heliyon, 9(9).

9

Global Finance Understanding International Monetary System

Monmath Gopal, Km Deepshikha and Ankit Kumar Shakya

Acharya Narendra Deva University of Agriculture and Technology Kumarganj Ayodhya, Uttar Pradesh

Abstract

The international monetary system serves as a critical framework for facilitating global trade, investment, and financial stability by establishing exchange rates, enabling currency conversions, and addressing economic imbalances and crises. Key components such as currencies, exchange rates, and reserve assets form its foundation, bolstered by international monetary institutions like the IMF and the World Bank. Recent trends, including the rise of digital currencies, regional monetary integration, and the impact of globalization. Digital currencies challenge traditional currency models, while regional monetary integration initiatives aim to enhance economic efficiency and stability. However, these efforts encounter obstacles such as potential loss of monetary independence. Cross-border trade has increased as a result of globalization, but it has also increased currency rate volatility, financial crises, and problems with sovereign debt, all of which need for efficient policy coordination and regulatory changes. Collaboration among policymakers, central banks, and global institutions is crucial to navigate these trends and ensure stability and prosperity for all stakeholders, paving the way for a future marked by inclusivity, sustainability, and economic resilience on a global scale.

Keywords: *International Monetary System, Global Trade, IMF, Exchange rate, Globalisation, Currencies, World Bank.*

Introduction

The international monetary system refers to the operating system of the financial environment, which consists of financial institutions, multinational corporations, and investors. It encompasses a set of regulations and norms designed to facilitate global trade and facilitate the movement of capital and investment between nations. It involves a network of government and financial institutions that establish exchange rates for different currencies. The evolution of this system is remarkable, considering its origins centuries ago when currency relied on gold coins and people engaged in bartering goods for trade. It's incredible how far the financial system has come from the days centuries ago, when the only form of money was gold coins, and transactions required bartering of goods or products for cash. The international monetary system provides financial support to nations in order to help them overcome debt and poverty. Inflation is a phenomenon that occurs when there is an excess of supply relative to demand.

Evolution of the International Monetary System

Prior to 1870, there was a bimetallic international monetary system, in which coins made of both gold and silver could be used as means of exchange. Each currency's gold or silver content governed the exchange rates between them. There were certain nations that used the gold or silver standard.

The British Empire ruled the economy and military during the 19th century. After the stabilization of the inflation brought on by the Napoleonic Wars, the United Kingdom adopted the gold standard in 1821. However, the remaining nations continued to adopt bimetallism, which involved using both gold and silver at different conversion ratios. The majority of European nations adopted the gold standard in the 1870s. With the return of price stability following the Civil War, the United States went back to the gold standard in 1879. In this sense, all of the main nations in Europe and North America were on the gold standard from 1879 until the abrupt start of World War I in July 1914. This indicated that their economies had a common financial mechanism, managed by the City of London financial market, and were thus mutually dependent. The gold standard ended in 1914 during World War I. Great Britain, France, Germany, and many other countries-imposed embargoes on gold exports and suspended redemption of bank notes in gold.

The interwar period was between World War I and World War II (1915-1944). Over this period, the United States replaced Britain as the leading financial power in the world. American gold standards were reinstated in 1919. While this was going on, several countries developed a gold sterilization policy, making sure that changes in credit and domestic currency balanced out gold imports and exports.

The International Monetary System (IMS) was founded in 1944 at a conference that took place in Bretton Woods, New Hampshire, in the United States. Participating nations agreed to uphold fixed exchange rates in relation to the US dollar, which was backed by gold, under this system. The International

Monetary Fund (IMF) was established to supervise the system and support member nations who were experiencing balance of payments issues. Additionally, the World Bank was founded to offer funding for development and reconstruction initiatives following a war. By linking currencies to the US dollar, which was itself backed by gold, the Bretton Woods system sought to foster stability in international monetary relations. But economic imbalances, especially the US trade deficit, which decreased US gold reserves, presented problems for the system. As a result, the Bretton Woods system eventually collapsed in the early 1970s. President Nixon essentially dismantled the fixed exchange rate regime when he declared in 1971 that the dollar would no longer be convertible to gold.

The flexible exchange rate regime emerged as a significant monetary system after the collapse of the Bretton Woods system in the early 1970s. Following the end of the Bretton Woods agreement, many countries shifted towards flexible exchange rates, allowing their currencies to float freely against each other. This move was driven by the recognition of the difficulties in maintaining fixed exchange rates amidst economic imbalances and the desire for greater policy autonomy. The adoption of flexible exchange rates gained momentum in the 1970s and 1980s, as countries sought to adjust to changing economic conditions and mitigate the impact of external shocks. During this period, several major economies, including the United States, Japan, and members of the European Economic Community, transitioned to floating exchange rates. Since then, the flexible exchange rate regime has become the dominant monetary system globally. Most countries today operate under some form of flexible exchange rate arrangement, either allowing their currencies to float freely or managing them within certain bands against a basket of other currencies. This system provides countries with greater flexibility to pursue independent monetary policies tailored to their domestic economic conditions, while also allowing exchange rates to adjust to external shocks and market forces.

Since 1985, the global economy has largely operated under a system of managed float exchange rates. This era emerged from the collapse of the Bretton Woods system, which had fixed exchange rates. Under managed float, currency values are determined by market forces but are subject to government intervention to stabilize fluctuations. Central banks employ various tools, such as interest rate adjustments and currency market interventions, to manage their currencies' values. This system allows for some flexibility while providing governments with a degree of control over their currency's exchange rate, aiming to promote economic stability and facilitate international trade and investment.

In current international financial system, the dollar is still the principal currency used in international transactions but its unchallenged dominance as an economic and financial force and Bretton Woods is dead but its child, the IMF, has evolved with the times and is more important than ever as watchdog and arbiter of balance of payments disequilibrium.

Importance

- The international monetary system provides a framework for conducting trade transactions by establishing exchange rates and facilitating currency conversions. This enables businesses and individuals to engage in cross-border trade and investment.
- A well-functioning international monetary system helps to reduce economic volatility by providing mechanisms for managing currency fluctuations, balance of payments issues, and financial crises. Stability in exchange rates and capital flows fosters confidence and encourages long-term investments.
- By promoting trade and investment flows, the international monetary system contributes to economic growth and development worldwide. It enables countries to access resources, technology, and markets, thereby enhancing productivity and prosperity.
- The international monetary system fosters financial integration by facilitating cross-border capital flows, investment diversification, and access to international financial markets. This integration enhances the efficiency of resource allocation and promotes financial market development.
- Cooperation among central banks and international monetary institutions within the system allows for coordinated monetary policies to address common challenges, such as inflation, unemployment, and financial instability. This coordination helps to maintain macroeconomic stability at the global level.
- Certain currencies, such as the US dollar and euro, serve as key reserve currencies in the international monetary system. These currencies are widely held by central banks as reserves, providing liquidity and stability to the global financial system.
- The international monetary system provides a platform for multilateral institutions like the International Monetary Fund (IMF) and the World Bank to address global economic imbalances, provide financial assistance to countries in need, and promote international cooperation in economic policymaking.
- Through mechanisms such as exchange rate adjustments, capital controls, and international financial assistance, the international monetary system

helps countries manage external imbalances, such as trade deficits or surpluses, and maintain overall economic equilibrium.[12]

Components of the Modern International Monetary System

Currencies and Exchange Rates

- **Currencies:** Each country issues its own currency, which serves as a medium of exchange within its borders. Examples include the US dollar, euro, Japanese yen, British pound, etc.
- **Exchange Rates:** Exchange rates determine the value of one currency relative to another. These rates fluctuate based on factors such as supply and demand, economic indicators, geopolitical events, and government policies. Exchange rates play a crucial role in facilitating international trade, investment, and capital flows.

Reserve Assets

- **Gold:** Historically, gold served as the primary reserve asset backing currencies. While no longer the primary reserve asset, central banks still hold significant gold reserves as a store of value and a hedge against economic uncertainties.
- **Special Drawing Rights (SDRs):** SDRs are international reserve assets created by the International Monetary Fund (IMF) to supplement its member countries' official reserves. SDRs are allocated to IMF member countries based on their quota subscriptions and can be used in international transactions.
- **Foreign Currencies:** Central banks hold reserves in foreign currencies, especially major currencies like the US dollar, euro, British pound, and Japanese yen. These reserves provide liquidity and stability to the domestic currency and facilitate international transactions and interventions in the foreign exchange market.

International Monetary Institutions

International Monetary Fund (IMF)

The IMF is a global financial institution established to promote international monetary cooperation, exchange rate stability, balanced growth, and financial stability. It provides financial assistance to member countries facing balance of payments problems, conducts surveillance of global economic developments, and offers policy advice and technical assistance. The International Monetary Fund (IMF) is a global financial institution with the primary mandate of promoting international monetary cooperation, exchange rate stability, balanced growth, and financial stability. Established in 1944, the IMF serves as a forum for member countries to collaborate on monetary policies and address common economic challenges. One of its key functions is to provide financial assistance to member countries facing balance of payments problems or experiencing economic crises. This assistance typically comes in the form of loans or credit lines aimed at restoring macroeconomic stability and fostering sustainable growth. Additionally, the IMF conducts surveillance of global economic developments, monitoring member countries' economic policies and performance to identify potential risks to the international monetary system. Through its surveillance activities, the IMF provides policy advice and technical assistance to help countries design and implement sound economic policies, strengthen institutional capacity, and address structural weaknesses in their economies.[7]

World Bank

The World Bank, comprising the International Bank for Reconstruction and Development (IBRD) and the International Development Association (IDA), stands as a pivotal international financial institution. Its primary mission is to provide loans and grants to developing nations for a wide array of development projects. These projects are meticulously designed to address pressing global challenges, with a strong emphasis on poverty reduction, sustainable development, and infrastructure enhancement. The IBRD primarily caters to middle-income and creditworthy low-income countries, offering them loans to support various development endeavours. Conversely, the IDA specializes in extending concessional financing, which includes grants and low-interest loans, to the world's poorest countries. Through its multifaceted support, the World Bank strives to uplift communities, foster economic growth, and elevate living standards across the globe. The World Bank is a key player in promoting positive change and long-term prosperity in developing nations through investments in vital areas including infrastructure, healthcare, education, and environmental sustainability. Its efforts are integral to achieving the Sustainable Development Goals (SDGs) and promoting inclusive and sustainable development worldwide.[9]

Global Financial Markets and Institutions

Foreign Exchange Market

The foreign exchange market is a decentralized global marketplace where currencies are bought and sold. It is the largest and most liquid financial market in the world, with daily trading volumes exceeding trillions of dollars. Participation in forex Market include commercial banks, central banks, hedge funds, multinational corporations, institutional investors, retail traders, and governments.

Functions: The primary function of the forex market is to facilitate currency conversion and international trade. It allows businesses and individuals to exchange one currency for another, enabling cross-border transactions. Additionally, the forex market serves as a platform for speculation, hedging, and arbitrage activities.

Instruments: The main instruments traded in the forex market are currency pairs, such as EUR/USD (Euro/US Dollar) and USD/JPY (US Dollar/Japanese Yen). Currency pairs are quoted in exchange rates, representing the relative value of one currency compared to another.

Capital Markets

Capital markets are financial markets where long-term debt and equity securities are bought and sold. These markets facilitate the issuance and trading of stocks, bonds, derivatives, and other financial instruments. Participation in capital markets include corporations, governments, institutional investors, retail investors, investment banks, and securities exchanges.

Functions: Capital markets play a crucial role in channelling funds from savers to borrowers, enabling businesses and governments to raise capital for investment and growth. They provide a platform for companies to issue stocks and bonds to finance operations and expansion projects. Additionally, capital markets offer investment opportunities for individuals seeking to grow their wealth through equity investments or fixed-income securities.

Instruments: Capital market instruments include stocks (equity securities), bonds (fixed-income securities), derivatives (options, futures, swaps), and other structured products. These instruments vary in risk and return characteristics, offering investors a diverse range of investment options.

Banking Institutions

Banking institutions encompass commercial banks, investment banks, central banks, and other financial institutions that provide various banking and financial services. Banking institutions are subject to regulatory oversight by government authorities to ensure financial stability, consumer protection, and adherence to prudential standards. Regulatory requirements may include capital adequacy ratios, liquidity requirements, risk management standards, and compliance with anti-money laundering (AML) and know-your-customer (KYC) regulations. It also plays a critical role in the economy by facilitating the efficient allocation of capital, providing liquidity, and supporting economic growth and development. They contribute to financial intermediation, payment systems, and monetary policy transmission, influencing economic activity and stability.

Functions: Banking institutions serve as intermediaries between depositors and borrowers, accepting deposits from individuals and businesses and lending funds to borrowers through loans and other credit products. They also offer a wide range of financial services, including checking and savings accounts, loans, mortgages, investment management, and advisory services.

Challenges in the International Monetary System

Exchange Rate Volatility

Exchange rate volatility refers to the degree of fluctuation or variability in the value of a currency relative to other currencies in the foreign exchange market. High levels of exchange rate volatility can create uncertainty and instability in international trade and investment. Exchange rate volatility can be caused by various factors, including economic fundamentals, geopolitical events, monetary policy decisions, interest rate differentials, speculation, market sentiment, and external shocks. Changes in these factors can lead to sudden and sharp movements in exchange rates. It can have significant consequences for businesses, investors, and policymakers. It can increase the costs and risks associated with international trade and investment, disrupt supply chains, affect profitability, and undermine macroeconomic stability. Moreover, exchange rate volatility can create challenges for central banks in conducting monetary policy and maintaining exchange rate stability.

To minimise exchange rate volatility, policymakers may implement measures such as exchange rate interventions, capital controls, monetary policy adjustments, and coordination among central banks. Businesses and investors can also use hedging strategies, such as forward contracts, options, and derivatives, to manage currency risk.

Financial Crises

Financial crises are events characterized by severe disruptions in financial markets and institutions, leading to widespread panic, asset price collapses, banking system failures, and economic downturns. Financial crises can have profound and long-lasting effects on economies, societies, and global financial stability. Financial crises can be triggered by various factors, including excessive leverage, asset bubbles, speculative bubbles, banking system weaknesses, inadequate regulation and supervision, macroeconomic imbalances, sudden shifts in investor sentiment, and contagion effects from other countries or regions. It can result in significant economic and social costs, including recessions, unemployment, poverty, inequality, fiscal deficits, sovereign debt defaults, currency devaluations, and political instability. They can also lead to financial contagion, spreading from one country to others through interconnected financial markets and institutions.

To reduce the risk of financial crises, policymakers may adopt measures such as strengthening financial regulation and supervision, enhancing crisis preparedness and management frameworks, improving transparency and disclosure standards, building robust financial infrastructure, implementing macroprudential policies, and fostering international cooperation and coordination.

Sovereign Debt Issues

Sovereign debt issues refer to challenges related to government borrowing and debt management, including issues such as excessive public debt, debt sustainability concerns, fiscal deficits, debt restructuring, and sovereign debt defaults. Sovereign debt issues can arise from factors such as fiscal mismanagement, unsustainable government spending, revenue shortfalls, economic downturns, currency depreciation, high interest rates, contingent liabilities, external shocks, and political instability. It also has serious consequences for countries, including higher borrowing costs, reduced investor confidence, credit rating downgrades, capital flight, currency depreciation, inflationary pressures, austerity measures, social unrest, and economic downturns.

To address sovereign debt issues, policymakers may implement measures such as fiscal consolidation, expenditure reforms, revenue enhancement, debt restructuring, debt relief initiatives, economic reforms, structural adjustments, and multilateral assistance programs from international financial institutions.

Recent Developments and Trends

Rise of Digital Currencies

Digital currencies, also known as cryptocurrencies or virtual currencies, are digital or virtual representations of value that use cryptography for security and operate independently of central banks or governments. The most well-known digital currency is Bitcoin, but there are thousands of other cryptocurrencies in existence. Over the past decade, digital currencies have gained significant traction and popularity, driven by technological advancements, increasing adoption by individuals and businesses, and growing interest from investors and financial institutions. Major developments include the emergence of blockchain technology, which underpins most cryptocurrencies, the creation of new digital assets and tokens for various purposes, and the integration of digital currency payments into mainstream financial systems. The rise of digital currencies has profound implications for the international monetary system. It challenges traditional models of currency issuance and monetary policy, introduces new forms of financial intermediation and payment systems, and raises regulatory and governance concerns regarding consumer protection, financial stability, money laundering, and illicit activities. Central banks and governments are exploring the potential benefits and risks of digital currencies and considering their own central bank digital currencies (CBDCs) to modernize payment systems and enhance financial inclusion.

Regional Monetary Integration

Regional monetary integration refers to the process by which countries in a specific geographic region coordinate their monetary policies, exchange rate arrangements, and financial systems to achieve greater economic integration and cooperation. In recent years, there has been a growing trend towards regional monetary integration, driven by economic globalization, trade liberalization, and regional economic blocs such as the European Union (EU), the African Union (AU), the Association of Southeast Asian Nations (ASEAN), and the Eurasian Economic Union (EAEU). These regional organizations have pursued various initiatives to harmonize monetary policies, establish common currency arrangements, and promote financial integration among member countries.

It has significant implications for the international monetary system. It can enhance economic efficiency, promote trade and investment, reduce transaction costs, and improve macroeconomic stability within the region. However, it also presents challenges such as asymmetric shocks, loss of monetary sovereignty, and governance issues. The success of regional monetary integration depends on effective coordination, institutional capacity, policy alignment, and political commitment among participating countries.

Impact of Globalization

Globalization refers to the increasing interconnectedness and interdependence of economies, societies, and cultures through cross-border flows of goods, services, capital, technology, and information. Globalization has accelerated in recent decades due to advances in technology, transportation, communication, and trade liberalization. This has led to the expansion of international trade and investment, the integration of financial markets, the emergence of global supply chains, and the movement of labour and capital across borders. However, globalization has also been accompanied by challenges such as income inequality, job displacement, environmental degradation, and financial instability. The impact of globalization on the international monetary system is profound and multifaceted. It has facilitated the spread of digital currencies, regional monetary integration initiatives, and global financial interconnectedness. However, it has also contributed to exchange rate volatility, financial crises, and sovereign debt issues, highlighting the need for effective policy coordination, regulatory reform, and international cooperation to promote sustainable economic development.

Conclusion

The international monetary system stands as a critical framework for global economic interactions, facilitating trade, investment, and financial stability across borders. By establishing exchange rates, providing mechanisms for currency conversions, and offering avenues for managing economic imbalances and crises, this system plays a pivotal role in fostering economic growth and development worldwide. Through mechanisms crafted by international monetary institutions like the IMF and the World Bank, nations find avenues for support, coordination, and resolution of economic challenges. Recent developments and trends, such as the rise of digital currencies, regional monetary integration, and the impacts of globalization, present both opportunities and challenges for the international monetary system. While digital currencies offer innovative solutions and potential benefits, they also raise regulatory concerns and require careful consideration. In this era of interconnectedness and interdependence, collaboration emerges as the guiding star, suggest the path towards stability and resilience. Policymakers, central banks, and international institutions must unite in a symphony of cooperation, transparency and inclusivity, crafting policies and frameworks that safeguard against volatility, crises and debt burdens. As they navigate the currents of change, embracing the opportunities that lie within while fortifying against the challenges that loom ahead, they pave the way towards a future marked by inclusivity, sustainability, and prosperity.

References

Bordo, M. D. (1993). The Bretton Woods international monetary system: a historical overview. In A retrospective on the Bretton Woods system: Lessons for international monetary reform (pp. 3-108). University of Chicago Press.

Claessens, M. S., & Kose, M. A. (2013). Financial crises explanations, types, and implications.

Dorrucci, E., & McKay, J. (2010). The international monetary system after the financial crisis. ECB Occasional paper, (123).

Elwell, C. K. (2011). Brief history of the gold standard (GS) in the United States.

Fritz, B., & Mühlich, L. (2006). Regional monetary integration among developing countries: new opportunities for macroeconomic stability beyond the theory of optimum currency areas.

https://www.elibrary.imf.org/display/book/9780300225631/ch006.xml

https://www.grips.ac.jp/teacher/oono/hp/lecture_F/lec01.htm

https://www.sciencedirect.com/topics/economics-econometrics-and-finance/international-monetary-system

https://www.worldbank.org/en/publication/wdr2022/brief/chapter-5-managing-sovereign-debt

Iqbal, J., Nosheen, M., & Wohar, M. (2023). Exchange rate volatility and India–US commodity trade: evidence of the third country effect. Indian Economic Review, 58(Suppl 2), 359-398.

Mussa, M., Masson, P., Swoboda, A., Jadresic, E., Mauro, P., & Berg, A. (2000). Exchange rate regimes in an increasingly integrated world economy (Vol. 193). Washington, DC: International Monetary Fund.

Perez-Saiz, H., Zhang, M. L., & Iyer, R. (2023). Currency Usage for Cross Border Payments. International Monetary Fund.

Pincus, J., & Winters, J. A. (Eds.). (2002). Reinventing the world bank. Cornell University Press.

Staff, I. M. F., Di Giovanni, J., Gottselig, G., Jaumotte, F., Ricci, L. A., & Tokarick, S. (2008). Globalization: A brief overview. International Monetary Fund, (02/08).

Vreeland, J. R. (2006). The International Monetary Fund (IMF): politics of conditional lending. Routledge.

10

Monetary Policy Steering The Economic Ship

Deep Narayan Yadav[1], Ankit Kumar Shakya[2], Ankit Tiwari[3] and Manaswini, N.[4]

[1,2]*Acharya Narendra Deva University of Agriculture and Technology, Kumarganj Ayodhya, Uttar Pradesh*

[3]*Acharya Narendra Deva University of Agriculture and Technology, Kumarganj Ayodhya, Uttar Pradesh*

[4]*Acharya Narendra Deva University of Agriculture and Technology, Kumarganj Ayodhya, Uttar Pradesh*

Abstract

Monetary policy is a critical tool for central banks to regulate economic activity, control inflation, and ensure financial stability. It involves various measures such as adjusting interest rates, managing the money supply, and influencing credit availability. However, the effectiveness of monetary policy is contingent upon factors like economic flexibility, growth dynamics, and inflation expectations. Central banks must navigate the intricate relationship between monetary policy and economic development, considering global economic influences and potential drawbacks. Money supply, categorized into monetary aggregates, is managed through tools like open market operations, reserve requirements, and interest rate adjustments. Expansionary policies aim to stimulate economic activity through increased money supply and lower interest rates, while contractionary policies aim to curb inflation by reducing the money supply and raising interest rates. Overall, central banks employ a mix of quantitative and qualitative measures to achieve their monetary policy objectives and maintain economic stability.

Keywords: *Monetary Policy, Money Supply, Interest Rates, Economic Growth, Central Banks*

Introduction

Monetary policies are the policies used to regulate the money supply, cost, and availability of credit in the economy. Monetary policy is considered as an important tool of controlling inflation in the economy.

Central banks use monetary policy to guide the economy. They set interest rates, control the amount of money in circulation, and take other actions to affect inflation, encourage economic growth, and ensure financial stability. The ability of monetary policy to influence the economy is not absolute. It is affected by several variables, such as how adaptable the economy can expand or contract (supply and demand) and the link between monetary policy and economic development. It plays a significant role in shaping the effectiveness of monetary policy. For example, when people have more pessimistic expectations of inflation, they tend to hold less money and monetize more debt. Economic growth tends to be positively correlated with certain financial factors. For instance, higher inflation, an increased money supply, and lower interest rates are often associated with stronger economic growth. Plus, people's expectations regarding future inflation can also impact economic growth. A reduction in available money can weaken the impact of monetary policy. To accurately assess the effectiveness of monetary policy, it's important to consider. Flexibility and limitations in economic supply and demand. The relationship between monetary policy and economic growth. Expectations of inflation It's also essential to account for potential drawbacks and unexpected effects of monetary policy. Additionally, monetary policy should consider the interaction between monetary and fiscal policies. In formulating domestic monetary policy, the global economic landscape holds significant sway. Factors such as the global economy, currency exchange rates, and international trade can profoundly influence a country's monetary policy framework. Moreover, in today's interconnected financial system, central banks must be cognizant of the broader implications their monetary actions may have on other economies, highlighting the need for a global perspective in monetary policy decision-making.

Need of Monetary Policy

Monetary policy plays a crucial role in maintaining stability and promoting economic growth. Monetary policy involves regulating interest rates and the money supply. It plays a crucial role in managing inflation, boosting investment and spending, and ensuring financial market stability. Additionally, monetary policy helps mitigate the adverse effects of economic shocks like recessions or financial crises. It can also influence expectations about inflation, which is vital for maintaining economic confidence. In essence, monetary policy aims to stabilize the economy, control inflation, promote growth, and bolster confidence in financial markets. By implementing suitable measures, monetary policy can balance inflation and unemployment rates, but with potential trade-offs.

Money

Money emerged to address the limitations of the barter system. In the past, people traded goods and services directly, facing challenges like the double coincidence of wants, where both parties had to desire each other's offerings. To overcome this, a standardized form of value, known as money, was created as a common medium of exchange.

Money and Near Money

Money and near money are terms used to describe different types of assets based on their liquidity and how easily they can be converted into cash. Here's a breakdown of each:

A. Money: Money is like a super-useful asset that we can use to buy and sell things (like a medium of exchange), measure the value of different things (like a unit of account), and save up for a rainy day (like a store of value). It's like a superpower that we can use every day. The most popular forms of money are: -

- **Currency:** Physical forms of money such as coins and banknotes issued by a government or central bank.
- **Demand Deposits:** Funds held in checking accounts or similar accounts that can be accessed quickly and without penalty.
- **Central Bank Reserves:** Deposits held by commercial banks at the central bank, which they use for interbank transactions and to meet reserve requirements.

Money is considered the most liquid form of wealth and is essential for facilitating daily transactions and economic activity.

B. Near Money: Near money encompasses assets that are less immediately accessible than actual cash but can be readily converted into money or used as a substitute for money with minimal hassle and waiting time. These assets are highly liquid but may involve some level of risk or transaction fees when exchanging them for cash. Examples include:

- **Savings Accounts:** Accounts held in banks or financial institutions that offer higher interest rates than checking accounts but still allow relatively easy access to funds.
- **Money Market Instruments:** Short-term debt securities with high liquidity and low risk, such as Treasury bills, commercial paper, and certificates of deposit (CDs).
- **Time Deposits:** Deposits held in savings accounts or CDs that require a fixed term or notice period before withdrawal but still offer some degree of liquidity.

Near money assets provide a balance between liquidity and return on investment, making them suitable for short-term savings or as a temporary store of value.

Characteristics of Money

- **Fungible currency:** For a currency to be effective, its units must be equal in value and can be exchanged seamlessly. If a currency does not meet this requirement, it becomes unreliable for use in transactions and is considered non-fungible.
- **Durable:** A good currency is durable enough to be used more than just one time. it must resist wear and tear, allowing for repeated use. Unlike perishable items that deteriorate over time, a currency should be durable to maintain its value and serve as a stable medium for future transactions. By ensuring durability, a currency preserves its long-term usefulness as a store of value and facilitator of exchange.
- **Easily recognizable:** It's crucial for users to trust that money is genuine. This means the currency should be widely recognized. If a currency is not recognized, there may be disputes about exchange rates. When a currency is recognized, it fosters trust in the monetary system and ensures it is accepted.
- **Stability:** For a currency to be effective, it must maintain a steady or growing value. A currency that fluctuates wildly is not sustainable. Dramatic value changes can undermine trust in the monetary system, making it less acceptable and reliable.
- **Portable:** For a currency to be effective, it should be: Portable: Easily carried and moved from place to place without significant inconvenience or cost. Divisible: Breakable into smaller units to enable transactions of varying amounts, making it convenient for different purchase sizes. Without divisibility, transportation costs for large sums could become prohibitive. Transferable: Easily moved from one person or place to another, allowing for seamless exchange and payments.

Functions of Money

Medium of exchange: Money is the generally accepted medium of exchange that is used to make all the transactions. Ex- payments of goods, payment of tax, etc.

A measure of Value: Money expresses the value of every service as well as goods. Therefore, it is a common denomination.

Standard of deferred payments: Money is considered the standard for future payments. Ex- The payment of the electricity bill on the upcoming due date.

Store of value: It means that money is capable of being stored and transferring the purchasing power from today to the future. Ex: Using the money in a savings account to buy new furniture.

Distribution of social income: Income can easily be distributed with the help of money. Ex: Distribution of total money earned by a school in the form of salaries, wages, utility bills, etc.

Basis of Credit Creation: The "store of value" function of the money helps in credit creation by the banks. Ex: Using the money of demand deposits as a tool for credit creation.

Liquidity: Money is the most liquid asset of the economy. Ex: Credit cards, debit cards, cash.

Types of Money

Money can take various forms depending on its attributes and functions within an economy. Here are some of the main types of money:

- **Commodity Money:** Commodity money is a type of currency that has inherent worth outside of its use as a medium of exchange. Throughout history, valuable items such as gold, silver, and rare metals have served as commodity money. These commodities possess intrinsic value because they are scarce, long-lasting, and useful in multiple sectors.
- **Fiat Money:** Fiat currency is money that is not backed by a tangible asset like gold or silver. Instead, it relies on the trust and faith people have in the government that issued it. This type of currency is commonly used today, with examples including the US dollar, euro, and Japanese yen. The government's responsibility is to maintain the value of this currency and ensure its widespread acceptance.
- **Representative Money:** Representative money is currency that stands in for a valuable item, typically a precious metal like gold or silver. Unlike commodity money, which can be traded directly for the item it represents, representative money allows you to exchange it for a set amount of the valuable item whenever you want. For instance, in the past when many countries used the gold standard, banknotes could be traded for a specific quantity of gold.
- **Cryptocurrency:** Cryptocurrencies are digital money that are digitally created and protected. They work on the internet with special codes to keep them safe. Nobody controls them, like the government or banks. Bitcoin, Ethereum, and Litecoin are some examples. They use a system called "blockchain" to remember who has what and to create new coins. Cryptocurrencies are popular because they aren't controlled by any one

group and people can use them to send money anywhere in the world easily.

- **Commercial Bank Money:** Commercial bank money is a type of money generated by banks through a practice known as fractional reserve banking. When a bank lends money, it essentially creates more money in the form of deposits in bank accounts. These electronic balances reside in customers' accounts and can be used for transactions within the banking network.
- **Electronic Money (E-Money):** E-money, or electronic money, exists solely in a digital format, eliminating physical cash. It's stored and exchanged entirely through electronic means. Examples of e-money include stored-value cards, mobile payment apps like Google Pay and Paytm, and online payment systems like Phone Pay. E-money has gained popularity for online shopping and personal transfers between individuals.

Money Supply

The total amount of money available in an economy at a specific time is called money supply. It encompasses physical money (coins and bills) and different forms of deposits in banks and other financial entities. Economists group money supply into categories called "monetary aggregates." These aggregates vary in size from narrow to broad, based on how easy it is to convert the money into cash.

Central banks in countries like the Federal Reserve or European Central Bank hold the power to manage the flow of money through monetary policies. These policies include:(a) Adjusting interest rates, (b) Purchasing or selling government bonds (open market operations), (c) Setting reserve levels for bank.

The size of the money available can greatly impact economic growth, inflation, and the interest rate. Central banks aim to manage the money supply to promote steady economic growth, keep inflation under control, and maintain financial stability. However, achieving these objectives can be challenging because the relationship between the money supply and other economic factors is complex and can be affected by multiple influences.

Concepts of Money Supply

- **Monetary Aggregates:** The amount of money in circulation is divided into different categories known as monetary aggregates. These categories vary based on how easily money can be used and accessed. The most common aggregates are: (a) M0: Physical currency held by the public, (b) M1: M0 + demand deposits (money in checking accounts) (c) M2: M1 + savings deposits, money market accounts, and other short-term deposits, (d) M3: M2 plus large time deposits and certain other assets.

- **Physical Currency (M0):** This represents the total amount of physical currency in circulation, including coins and banknotes held by the public and in the vaults of commercial banks.
- **M1:** M1 is a basic measure of the money supply, encompassing physical cash (M0) and demand deposits. Demand deposits are funds stored in checking accounts or other accounts that allow immediate access, like traveller's checks.
- **M2:** M2 is a larger measure of the money supply than M1. It includes M1 as well as other types of assets that are not as easily convertible into cash or used for payment but can be made liquid more quickly than long-term investments. Examples of these assets include savings accounts, money market mutual funds, and time deposits with a specified maturity date.
- **M3:** M3 is a monetary measure that's more comprehensive than M2. It encompasses M2 components, as well as additional larger time deposits, institutional money market funds, and other highly liquid assets.

Minimum Reserve System

Central banks use the minimum reserve system to control the amount of money available in the economy and impact economic conditions. Commercial banks are obligated to maintain a specific portion of their customer deposits as reserves, which can be either cash or money deposited with the central bank.

Credit control Measures

These are measures used by central government to control the credit flow in the economy. The credit control measures are classified into three types visually: -

- Quantitative measures
- Qualitative measures
- Other measures

Quantitative Measures

Cash reserve ratio

The central bank uses the cash reserve ratio (CRR) to control the money supply. It requires banks to keep a specific percentage of their deposits (as cash or deposits with the central bank). By adjusting the CRR, the central bank can impact the amount of money available for banks to lend. Lowering the

CRR makes more money available for lending, increasing the money supply and potentially boosting economic activity. Raising the CRR reduces lending funds, contracting the money supply and slowing economic growth.

Banks are required to maintain a specific portion of their demand deposits, including net demand and time liabilities, in cash with the Reserve Bank of India (RBI) always. This percentage is typically not eligible for interest accrual.

Statutory Liquid Ratio

The Statutory Liquidity Ratio (SLR) is a mandatory portion of a bank's deposits that must be set aside in specific liquid assets, including cash, gold, and government-backed securities. This requirement is established by the central bank or government to regulate the financial system. The main goal of SLR is to ensure that banks can fulfil their short-term commitments and remain stable, thereby protecting depositors and maintaining the soundness of the financial system. Banks must follow Statutory Liquidity Ratio (SLR) guidelines set by central banks. Not meeting SLR requirements can result in penalties or other actions. SLR is used by central banks as a monetary policy tool to control the economy's money supply and credit. By changing SLR requirements, central banks affect the money available for commercial bank lending, impacting liquidity and economic activity.

Open Market Operations

Open market operations involve central banks buying or selling government-issued securities in the public market to influence the amount of money in circulation, interest rates, and the broader economy. Unlike direct negotiations, these transactions occur publicly. The goal is to align with the central bank's monetary policy objectives, such as controlling inflation, managing interest rates, or stimulating economic growth. The central bank can influence the money supply through the buying and selling of government bonds. Buying bonds adds money to banks' reserves, which boosts lending and economic activity. Conversely, selling bonds reduces bank reserves, restricting lending and potentially slowing economic growth.

Central banks use open market operations to control short-term interest rates in the economy. By buying government bonds, the central bank makes them more in demand, causing their prices to rise and yields (interest rates) to fall. Conversely, selling bonds increases the supply, lowering prices and raising yields. This flexibility allows central banks to make small but precise adjustments to monetary policy to meet changing economic conditions and achieve their policy goals, making open market operations a crucial tool in monetary policy.

Bank Rate

The bank rate, often called the discount or policy rate, is the interest rate charged by a central bank when it lends money to other banks and financial institutions. Central banks use the bank rate as a tool to control the economy. They set the rate to meet specific goals, such as keeping prices stable, promoting economic growth, or ensuring the stability of the financial system. Changes in the bank rate directly impact how much it costs to borrow and lend money, leading to ripple effects throughout the economy. Banks can get money from the central bank to help with short-term funding or liquidity shortages. They do this through different methods, like the discount window and overnight lending. When the central bank raises its bank rate, banks have to pay more to borrow, which leads to higher interest rates for businesses and consumers. On the other hand, when the bank rate goes down, it's cheaper for banks to borrow, which encourages them to lend more and boosts the economy.

Changes in the bank rate, set by central banks, impact the economy by affecting the availability and cost of money. An increase in the bank rate generally reduces the supply of money and credit because borrowing becomes more expensive. This slowdown in lending can lead to lower economic activity. In contrast, a decrease in the bank rate expands the money supply and encourages borrowing and investment, potentially stimulating economic growth. Central banks use bank rate changes to signal their monetary policy approach and to influence financial markets and the public. By providing guidance on future bank rate changes, central banks can shape market expectations and guide financial decision-making.

Liquidity Adjustment Facility

The Liquidity Adjustment Facility (LAF) helps central banks, like the Reserve Bank of India (RBI), control liquidity in the banking system over the short term. It's a tool used to manage how much money is available to banks. The goal is to make sure there's enough money for banks to operate smoothly while also keeping inflation and interest rates stable. This helps the central bank achieve its financial stability goals.

- **Components:** The Liquidity Adjustment Facility typically consists of two main components: the repo rate and the reverse repo rate.
- **Repo Rate:** Banks can borrow money for a short period from the central bank through the repo rate. To do this, they sell the central bank securities (like government bonds) with a promise to buy them back later. Banks use this repo facility to get cash from the central bank by using these securities as collateral. This helps banks meet their short-term cash requirements.

- **Reverse Repo Rate:** Banks can temporarily place excess funds with the central bank through a process called reverse repo. In this transaction, banks lend securities to the central bank and receive funds in exchange. Banks utilize this facility to generate income from their idle funds while holding onto the deposited securities.

Central bank actions regarding the repo rate and reverse repo rate have a significant impact on short-term interest rates and the amount of money available in the economy. Raising the repo rate makes borrowing more expensive, reducing the supply of money and potentially slowing down economic expansion. On the other hand, lowering the repo rate encourages borrowing and economic activity.

Marginal Standing Facility

The Marginal Standing Facility (MSF), created by the Reserve Bank of India (RBI), enables banks to borrow short-term funds from the RBI. To qualify for this facility, banks must have used up their borrowing limit under the Liquidity Adjustment Facility (LAF) or are experiencing unexpected funding shortages. The MSF serves as an emergency lending tool for banks, providing them with access to funds at an interest rate higher than the standard repo rate to cover their immediate liquidity requirements. Typically, borrowing money through the Marginal Standing Facility (MSF) comes with a higher interest rate than the repo rate. The Reserve Bank of India (RBI) sets the MSF rate, which is generally a fixed percentage above the repo rate. This higher rate encourages banks to use the MSF as a last resort, preventing overuse of emergency borrowing. To obtain funds through the MSF, banks can offer suitable securities like government bonds or other high-quality assets as collateral. The central bank determines the acceptable securities and their criteria for accessing the MSF. Banks often turn to the Marginal Standing Facility (MSF) when they don't have enough cash and can't borrow money from other sources like the repo market or other banks. The MSF offers banks a dependable source of funds to cover their short-term financial needs and ensure smooth operations.

Qualitative Measures

Credit rationing

Selective credit controls include rationing, which regulates the use of loans by banks. There are four main types of rationing: 1. Variable Portfolio Ceiling: The central bank sets a maximum limit on total loans that banks can issue. 2.Variable Capital Assets Ratio: The central bank sets a ratio between a bank's capital and its total assets. This ratio can be adjusted to limit or expand lending. 3. Selective Credit Controls: The central bank can direct banks to restrict lending in specific sectors or industries to achieve specific economic objectives. 4.Credit Card Controls: The central bank can implement regulations on credit card issuance and usage to manage consumer spending and credit risk. The third technique discriminates against larger banks by limiting their lending capacity more than smaller banks. Additionally, by controlling credit for specific objectives, the central bank loses its status as the lender of last resort.

Margin Requirement

This method is employed to prevent excessive use of credit to purchase or carry securities by speculators. The central bank fixes minimum margin requirements on loan for purchasing and carrying securities. They are in fact the percentage of the value of the security that cannot be borrowed or lent. In other words, it is the maximum value of loan which a borrower can have from the banks based on the security. For example, if a central bank fixes a 10% margin on the value of the security worth Rs 1000, then the commercial bank can lend only Rs 900 to the holder of the security and keep Rs 100 with it.

Regulation of Consumer Credit

This is another method of selective credit control which aims at the regulation of consumer instalment credit or hire purchase finance. The main objective of this instrument is to regulate the demand of durable consumer goods in the interest of economic stability. The central bank regulates the use of bank credit by consumers in order to buy durable consumer goods on instalment and hire purchase. For this purpose, it employs two devices: minimum downpayments and maximum period of repayments.

Differential Rate of Interest

Central bank fixes the different rate of or interest ceiling for different sectors. Interest subvention scheme for agricultural loan.

Other Measures

Moral Suasion

Moral suasion in the method of persuasion, of request, of informal suggestion, and of advice to the commercial banks usually adopted by the central bank. To executive head of the central bank calls a meeting of the heads of the commercial banks wherein he explains them the need for the adoption of a particular monetary policy in the context of the current economic situation, and then appeals to them to follow it.

Direct Action

Central bank in all countries frequently resort to direction action against commercial banks. Direction action is in the form of directives issued from time to time to the commercial banks to follow a particular policy which a central bank wants to enforce immediately. This policy may not be used against all banks but against erring banks. For example, monetary penalty, sanctions, etc.

Types of Monetary Policies

Expansionary Monetary Policy

Central banks use expansionary monetary policy to boost economic activity and increase demand. By pumping more money into the economy, lowering interest rates, and making it easier to borrow money, this strategy encourages businesses and consumers to spend more.

Central banks can cut the interest rates they charge commercial banks for loans. This makes borrowing more affordable for businesses and individuals, leading to increased spending and borrowing, as well as higher levels of investment.

Central banks can boost the economy by buying government bonds in the open market. This action increases the money supply by adding funds to commercial bank reserves. Consequently, commercial banks can extend more loans to businesses and individuals, stimulating economic activity.

Central banks can boost lending and economic growth by reducing the reserve requirement, the amount of money banks are legally required to keep on hand. When this requirement is lowered, banks have more money to lend, which can lead to increased spending and investment.

Central banks can communicate their plans for future policy adjustments through "forward guidance." By clearly stating their commitment to fostering economic growth and keeping a loose monetary environment, they can shape market expectations and stimulate borrowing and spending.

When faced with severe economic challenges, central banks may resort to quantitative easing. This measure involves acquiring vast amounts of government bonds and securities. The purpose of this action is twofold: to expand the money supply and reduce interest rates over extended periods.

Contractionary Monetary Policy

Central banks implement contractionary monetary policies to decrease the amount of money in circulation and curb inflation or excessive economic growth. This strategy includes raising interest rates, constricting the money supply, or tightening credit standards. By increasing interest rates, borrowing becomes more costly for businesses and individuals, discouraging their spending and borrowing. This slowdown in economic activity and reduced demand can help alleviate inflationary pressures.

Central banks can reduce the money supply through two methods: (a) Selling government bonds(b) Selling bonds to businesses or individuals withdraws money from circulation. When banks buy these bonds, they use their reserves to do so, which reduces the money available for loans. Increasing reserve requirements, Central banks can increase the amount of money banks must keep as reserves instead of lending. This reduces the amount of money banks can loan out, further decreasing the money supply.

Central banks can guide economic behaviour by indicating their plans for future monetary policies. By clearly stating their dedication to keeping inflation under control and ensuring stable prices, these banks can shape expectations in the market and prevent inflation from spiralling out of control. The central bank is downsizing its asset holdings by selling off previously acquired assets. This action reduces the excess funds (reserves) available to banks, making it harder for them to lend and borrow money.

Conclusion

Monetary policy, controlled by central banks, is all about managing two main things: how much money is floating around in the economy and the cost of borrowing that money, known as interest rates. Central banks use these tools to achieve a few big goals: boosting economic growth, keeping prices stable (controlling inflation), and making sure the financial system stays strong. They do this by adjusting the amount of money in circulation and changing interest rates. For example, when the economy needs a boost, central banks can increase the amount of money available by buying government securities, making it cheaper for people and businesses to borrow money. This encourages spending and investment, which can help the economy grow. Conversely, when prices are rising too fast (inflation), central banks may raise interest rates to make borrowing more expensive, which helps to slow down spending and keep prices stable. However, the success of these actions depends on how flexible the economy is and what's happening in the wider world economy. Flexible economies can respond more easily to changes in monetary policy, while global factors like trade and currency movements can complicate matters. Despite these challenges, central banks play a crucial role in steering economies towards stability and prosperity through their careful management of monetary policy.

References

Abbas, K., & Fazal, H. (2006). Money, Income and Prices in Pakistan, A Bi-variat and Tri-varate Causility. MPRA Paper 4892, University Library of Munich, Germany

Ahmed, A. E. M., & Suliman, S. Z. (2011). The Long-Run relationship between money supply, Real GDP and price level: Empirical evidence from Sudan. Journal of Business Studies Quarterly, 2(2), 68-79.

Ben, S. B.; Fredric, S. M. (1997). Inflation Targeting: A New Framework for Monetary Policy. Journal of Economic perspectives,11(2); pp.97-116.

Ben, S. B.; Gertler, M. (2000) Monetary Policy and Asset Price Volatility. National Bureau of Economic Research, Working Paper no. 7559.

Bhattacharya, J., Singh, R., (2008). Optimal choice of monetary policy instruments in an economy with real and liquidity shocks. Journal of Economic Dynamics and Control, 32(4), 1273-1311.

Brunner, K. and Meltzer, A. (1971). 'The uses of money: money in the theory of an exchange economy' American Economic Review, Vol. 65, No. 5, pages 784–805.

Budina, N., Maliszewski, W., De Menil, G., & Turlea, G. (2006). Money, inflation and output in Romania,1992–2000. Journal of International Money and Finance, 25(2), 330-347.

Handa, J., (2009). Monetary Economics (2nd ed.). Oxford: Routledge.

Maurer, B. (2006) The Anthropology of Money. Annu. Rev. Anthropol, 35:15-36.

Menger, C. (1892), 'On the origins of money', Economic Journal, Vol. 2, No. 6, pages 239–55.

Ramli, R. (2014). Inflation, Money Supply and Economic Growth: A Causality Analysis for Malaysia. Journal of the Department of Statistics. Vol 1, 17-29.

Shrestha, B. (2010). Impact of Money Supply on GDP and Price: Case of Nepal.

Singh, R., Subramanian, C., (2008). The optimal choice of monetary policy instruments in a small open economy. Canadian Journal of Economics/Revue canadienne d'économique, 41(1), 105-137.

11

The Future of Finance Trends, Predictions, and Preparations

Shiv Kumar Rana[1], Sandeep Gautam[2] and Prateek Kumar[3]

[1]Department of Agricultural Statistics, Acharya Narendra Deva University of Agriculture and Technology, Kumarganj, Ayodhya, Uttar Pradesh

[2]Department of Agricultural Economics, Acharya Narendra Deva University of Agriculture and Technology, Kumarganj, Ayodhya, Uttar Pradesh

[3]Department of Extension Education, Acharya Narendra Deva University of Agriculture and Technology, Kumarganj, Ayodhya, Uttar Pradesh

Abstract

The future of finance is influenced by technological advancements, consumer behaviour, and global economic changes. Key trends include automation, data-driven decision-making, block chain integration, fintech innovation, and inclusive services. Predictions for 2025 emphasize digital transformation, disruptive technologies like AI and block chain, and a clear strategy. Preparations involve redefining finance professionals' roles, leveraging technology for efficiency, and fostering innovation within organizations. The future of finance will be characterized by a blend of technology-driven solutions, strategic foresight, and agile responses to emerging trends.

Keywords: *Block chain, Artificial intelligence (AI), Machine learning, Crypto currency, Cloud banking.*

Introduction

The world of finance revolves around the management, generation, and analysis of money and investment opportunities. Financial professionals orchestrate a complex dance involving credit, borrowing, and various investment instruments like securities and stocks. This intricate choreography aims to fund present endeavours using a strategic allocation of anticipated future income. Since finance deals with the flow of money across time, grasping the time value of money is essential. Understanding interest rates and how they impact investments becomes paramount for making sound financial decisions that consider both present needs and future goals. This intricate web of concepts is what finance professionals navigate to ensure the optimal use of financial resources. Finance can be broadly divided into three types:

1. Public finance
2. Corporate finance
3. Personal finance

1. Public Finance: The government steps in to prevent the economy from going off track by managing how resources are distributed, income is shared fairly, and the economy remains stable. Taxes are the main way the government gets the money to fund these programs. Borrowing from banks, insurance companies, and even other countries, along with any profits from government-owned businesses, also contributes to the government's financial resources. State and local governments get money in a few ways:

- **Federal gifts:** They sometimes get money from the federal government.
- **Fees:** They charge for things you use, like parking or using the airport.
- **Fines:** They get money from tickets and fines.
- **Licenses:** They charge fees for licenses, like your driver's permit.
- **Borrowing:** They can borrow money to pay for things.

2. Corporate Finance: Businesses receive finance in several ways, ranging from stock investments to credit agreements. A business may obtain a bank loan or set up a line of credit. Acquiring and managing debt effectively may help a business grow and become more profitable.

Angel investors and venture capitalists may provide funds to startups in return for a stake in the business. A successful business will issue shares on a stock market upon becoming public, and these initial public offerings (IPOs) significantly increase a company's cash flow. To raise money, well-established businesses could issue corporate bonds or sell more shares. To increase revenue, businesses might acquire interest-bearing bank certificates of deposit (CDs), dividend-paying equities, or blue-chip bonds. They can even buy other businesses.

A few recent instances of company finance are as follows:

- Bausch & Lomb Corp. filed for an IPO on January 13, 2022, and sold shares formally in May of the same year. The medical business made $630 million in revenue.
- In order to raise capital or pay off debt, Ford Motor Credit Company LLC manages outstanding notes.
- Home Light, a real estate company, raised $115 million through a blended finance strategy, which consisted of $60 million from the

issuance of additional equity and $55 million from debt financing. Home Light utilized the extra funds to purchase startup loans. Acknowledge. inc

3. Personal Finance: Personal financial planning often entails assessing a person's or family's present financial situation, projecting both short- and long-term requirements, and carrying out a plan to satisfy those wants while staying within the person's means. A person's salary, standard of life, and personal objectives and preferences all have a major role in their personal finances.

Personal finance issues encompass a wide range of topics, such as obtaining financial goods such as credit cards, home and life insurance, mortgages, and retirement plans. Personal finance also includes personal banking, which includes 401(k) plans, individual retirement accounts (IRAs), and checking and savings accounts.

The following are the key components of personal finance:

- Determining an individual's existing financial situation (anticipated cash flow, savings, etc.)
- Purchasing insurance to guard against risk and guarantee one's material well-being.
- Calculating and filing taxes
- Allocating savings and investments
- And making retirement plans

Although variations of personal finance have been taught in colleges and universities under the names "home economics" and "consumer economics" since the early 20th century, the topic is relatively new. At first, men economists ignored the topic because they thought "home economics" was a domain best left to housewives. Economists have been emphasizing lately how important it is for everyone to be financially literate to ensure the macroeconomic health of the country as a whole.

The challenges and disruptions in the present financial state

It's a perfect storm for the finance function, and even the most seasoned CFOs are finding their mettle tested. The financial teams are confronted with a plethora of difficulties that need flexibility, inventiveness, and nimbleness, ranging from the COVID-19 outbreak to digital change. In the current corporate environment, the following are some of the major interruptions that finance departments must deal with:

1. **Digital Transformation:** The digital transformation is rapidly advancing, and finance departments need to stay up to date with emerging

technology to avoid falling behind. The tools available to us, such as block chain, AI, and ML, have enormous potential for productivity, understanding, and development. However, they also call for a radical rethinking of established financial procedures and the development of new skill sets.

2. **Economic Uncertainty:** The world economy is more unstable than it has ever been, with risk and uncertainty being fuelled by variables including currency swings, trade conflicts, and unstable political environments. Finance teams in this context have to strike a balance between the necessity of risk management and financial stability and the requirement for strategic investments and development.
3. **Cybersecurity Threats:** Cyber-attacks, data breaches, and hacking are just a few of the new security risks that have emerged with the advent of digital technology. For firms, these risks can have disastrous repercussions, including harm to their brand and even financial loss. Finance teams need to collaborate closely with IT and security specialists to protect systems and data because of these dangers.
4. **Talent Acquisition:** Locating the correct expertise has gotten increasingly difficult as the financial function grows more specialized and sophisticated. In a crowded and competitive market, CFOs must fight for top personnel while advancing their current teams to meet evolving needs.
5. **Regulatory Compliance:** The complexity and strictness of regulations and compliance requirements are rising, especially in sectors like healthcare and finance. CFOs are responsible for making sure their staffs are informed on the most recent laws and regulations. To comply with these standards, financial departments will need to have the appropriate systems and procedures in place.
6. **COVID-19 Pandemic:** With finance teams leading the front lines of the response, the COVID-19 epidemic has been a seismic event for corporations. CFOs have to navigate a constantly changing environment and make important decisions in the face of uncertainty in a variety of areas, including managing cash flow, financial reporting, and scenario planning. In addition to being difficulties, these disruptions present you with chances to innovate and change for the better. But in order to do this, you'll need to be prepared to try new things, take chances, and always learn and grow.

Digital Innovation

Digital innovation is driving big changes in the future of finance. Important trends, predictions, and preparations include:

1. **Fintech and digitalization:** Fintech and digitalization are now linked, with digital transformation transforming the financial industry. The use of digital technology is driving this change, which makes financial services more efficient, inventive, and focused on the needs of their customers. Fintech businesses are using digital tools like automation, block chain, AI, and mobile banking to improve consumer experiences, expedite workflows, and spur industry expansion. The notable influence of digitalization on Fintech is seen in the swift expansion of digital banking, the emergence of machine learning instruments, and the growing acceptance of digital transformation programs in the financial sector. In the rapidly changing digital era of finance, this move towards digitization is changing the financial environment, increasing operating efficiency, cutting costs, and improving client engagement.
2. **Artificial Intelligence (AI):** Creating computer systems that are capable of activities that normally require human intelligence is known as artificial intelligence (AI). It entails creating hardware and software that can simulate how people think in order to make decisions, evaluate information, and engage with their surroundings. AI includes several subfields, including robotics, machine learning, deep learning, and natural language processing.
3. **Machine learning (ML):** Creating algorithms that can learn from data to make predictions, spot trends, and enhance performance over time is the goal of machine learning, a subset of artificial intelligence. Models that can carry out complicated tasks without explicit programming are created by ML algorithms through dataset training. This technique, which falls under the larger category of artificial intelligence, allows computers to gain new skills and capabilities by learning from data and experience.
4. **Block chain and crypto currencies:** New technologies are changing the way people transfer money and stay secure. Block chain technology is improving security and efficiency in financial operations while speeding up touch less transaction. Block chain technology and crypto currencies are closely related; block chain powers crypto currencies like Ethereum and Bitcoin.

5. **Decentralization and Security:** Since crypto currencies operate on dispersed public ledgers like block chains, a central authority is not required to validate transactions. Transactions are more private and secure because to its decentralized structure, which makes them more secure than conventional debit/credit card transactions. Because block chain networks are transparent, anybody can observe and validate transactions, which lowers the possibility of fraud or manipulation.
6. **Cloud Banking:** By storing and processing financial data remotely via cloud technology, this approach provides flexibility, cost-effectiveness, and enhanced data security. Organizations may reduce operational costs, manage data efficiently, and access global resources using cloud banking.
7. **Embedded Finance:** Enhancing loans and other financial services, such digital payments, via the use of digital technology. This technology increases productivity, reduces expenses, and streamlines the provision of financial services by integrating financial services across several platforms and apps.
8. **Robotic Process Automation (RPA):** In the financial services industry, tasks and processes are automated via the use of robots, software, and algorithms. RPA increases operational efficiency by doing away with manual labour in jobs like fraud detection, reconciliation, and payment processing.

Advantages of Future of Finance

Based on the trends, predictions, and preparation described in the references given, the finance sector has several benefits in the future:

1. **Enhanced Transparency and Value:** Through collaborations, cutting-edge products, and better customer experiences, the banking industry is advancing toward more transparency and value creation.
2. **Strategic Planning and Forecasting:** By incorporating non-financial data into planning, budgeting, and forecasting procedures, businesses may achieve better results, more precise forecasts, and increased levels of confidence and trust among stakeholders.
3. **Integration of Innovative technology:** Adopting cutting-edge technology such as artificial intelligence (AI), cloud computing, and data analytics may simplify operations, cut expenses, reveal business prospects, and build a more integrated financial ecosystem.

4. **Cross-Functional Collaboration:** By working with other departments to foster innovation, up skill teams, and deploy innovative solutions with a people-first mentality, finance executives are progressively evolving into strategic advisers to the business.
5. **Financial Inclusion and Accessibility:** To promote financial inclusion and improve accessibility, financial services will need to be expanded into a variety of industries, including healthcare, transportation, human resources, and education.
6. **Adaptability and Resilience:** An adaptable finance function with a wide range of skills can react swiftly to difficulties by anticipating unforeseen events and handling change in a comprehensive way [12].
7. **Data-Driven Decision-Making:** Staying ahead of changing company demands, planning for different situations, and making educated decisions may all be facilitated by relying on data insights and market observations.

Conclusion

The financial sector has a bright future ahead of it, but it is also evolving quickly. Financial institutions will need to adopt new technology, adhere to evolving laws, and adjust to shifting customer demands in order to stay ahead of the curve. The sector is being disrupted by the emergence of fintech startups and other new competitors, but it is also opening new avenues for innovation and expansion. To make sure that your company remains competitive and relevant in the ever-evolving financial sector, it is critical that we monitor new developments and forecasts.

It's certain that new trends and technological advancements will continue to influence the banking sector in novel and fascinating ways as we look to the future. Keeping abreast with the most recent trends and forecasts is essential to being ahead of the curve. The programs offered by ICOFP are tailored to provide you with the necessary knowledge and abilities to prosper in a dynamic business. We invite you to look around our website or get in touch with us if you have any questions. Gaining the information and abilities necessary to be successful in the finance sector of the future is possible with ICOFP.

References

https://www.investopedia.com/terms/f/finance.asp#toc-what-is-finance

https://www2.deloitte.com/us/en/pages/finance-transformation/articles/finance-digital-transformation-for-cfos.html

https://www.expensein.com/blog/business-advice/finance-digital-transformation

https://www.linkedin.com/pulse/how-prepare-future-trends-financial-services-giovanni-sisinna

https://appinventiv.com/blog/change-in-fintech-using-digital-transformation/
https://www.linkedin.com/pulse/how-digital-transformation-revolutionizing-fintechindustry
https://ai.engineering.columbia.edu/ai-vs-machine-learning/
https://mitsloan.mit.edu/ideas-made-to-matter/machine-learning-explained
https://www.coursera.org/articles/machine-learning-vs-ai
https://www.coinbase.com/learn/crypto-basics/what-is-a-blockchain
https://www.forbes.com/advisor/investing/esg-investing/
https://www.oecd.org/finance/esg-investing.htm
https://www.investopedia.com/terms/e/environmental-social-and-governance-esg-criteria.asp
https://www.ibm.com/downloads/cas/KNVLN4DY
https://www2.deloitte.com/us/en/pages/finance-transformation/articles/future-finance-trends-2025.html
https://www.icofp.org/blog/future-finance-industry-trends-predictions/

12

Understanding Economics Cycle Recession Recovery and Beyond

Mahima Priyanka Neerugatti[1], Aditya Bhooshan Srivastava[2] Sachin Kumar Verma[3] and Deep Chand Nishad[4]

[1,2,3]Acharya Narendra Deva University of Agriculture and Technology, Kumarganj Ayodhya, Uttar Pradesh

[4]Acharya Narendra Deva University of Agriculture and Technology, Kumarganj Ayodhya, Uttar Pradesh

Abstract

The economic cycle, or business cycle, encompasses the fluctuating pattern of economic activity, impacting vital indicators like GDP, employment, and consumer spending. Understanding its phases—expansion, peak, contraction, and trough—is pivotal for stakeholders to navigate investment decisions and policymaking. Expansion is marked by increased production, lower unemployment, higher wages, and consumer spending, while contraction sees the opposite. Peaks represent the apex of expansion, potentially leading to overheating and inflation, while troughs denote economic lows typified by reduced income, high unemployment, and diminished demand. Recovery follows troughs, signaling optimism and growth. Economic cycles, exemplified by historical events like the Great Depression and recent crises, are measured through GDP, unemployment rates, and other indicators. Internal factors like demand fluctuations and external factors like wars shape these cycles. Businesses, influenced by cycle phases, adjust production, investment, and pricing strategies accordingly. Factors such as interest rates and consumer sentiment also sway economic trends. Understanding these dynamics aids businesses in making informed decisions to navigate the ever-changing economic landscape.

Keywords: *Economic cycle, expansion, contraction, peak, depression*

Introduction

The economic cycle, also known as the business cycle, refers to the fluctuating state of an economy characterized by periods of economic expansion and contraction. It involves the cyclical pattern of growth and decline in economic activity, impacting various indicators like gross domestic product (GDP), employment rates, interest rates, and consumer spending[2]. The economic cycle is a fundamental concept in economics that helps determine the overall state of an economy as it moves through four distinct stages: expansion, peak, contraction, and trough. Understanding the economic cycle is crucial for investors, businesses, and policymakers as it influences investment decisions, business strategies, and economic policies based on the prevailing stage of the cycle.

"According to Arthur Burns and Wesley Mitchell business cycle are a type of fluctuation found in the aggregate economic activity of nations that they organize their work mainly in business enterprises".

Phases of Business Cycle

1. **Expansion**
2. **Peak**
3. **Contraction**
4. **Trough/Depression**

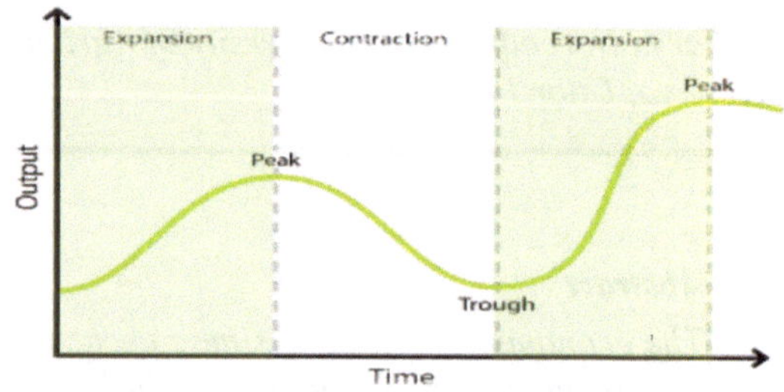

1. Expansion

The upswing of the business cycle towards a peak is called an economic expansion. An economic expansion is associated with:

Firstly, an increase in production and output is a prominent feature of economic expansion. This uptick in production signifies growing economic activity, as businesses ramp up their operations to meet rising demand.

Additionally, economic expansions are typically associated with a decrease in unemployment rates. As businesses expand and demand for goods and services rises, job opportunities increase, leading to a decline in unemployment levels[1].

Moreover, economic expansions often coincide with an increase in wages as labour markets tighten due to higher demand for workers. This rise in wages reflects improved economic conditions and the ability of workers to negotiate better pay.

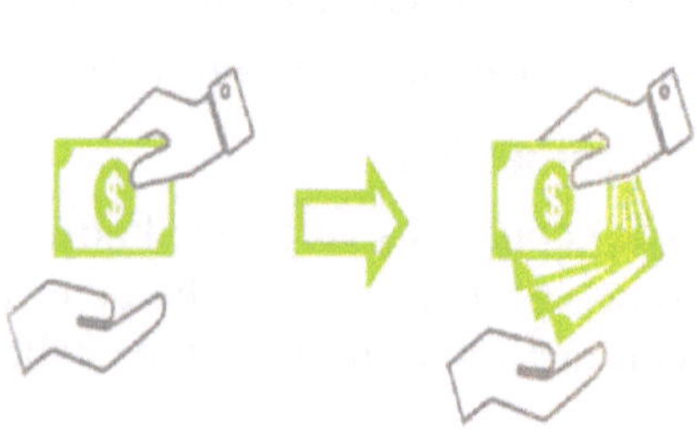

Lastly, economic expansions are marked by an increase in consumer spending. With more people employed, earning higher wages, and feeling optimistic about the economy, consumer confidence grows, leading to higher spending on goods and services.

2. Contraction

The downswing of the business cycle towards a trough, known as an economic contraction, is characterized by several key indicators.

Firstly, there is a decrease in production/output during this phase, reflecting a slowdown in economic activity and reduced output of goods and services.

Additionally, an increase in unemployment is a common feature of an economic contraction, as businesses may cut back on hiring or even lay off workers due to decreased demand and production.

Moreover, a decrease in wages is often observed as businesses face challenges in maintaining previous salary levels amidst economic downturns. Workers are willing to accept lower wages, as the increase in unemployment has meant there is more competition for jobs.

Lastly, a decrease in consumer spending is prevalent during an economic contraction as individuals and households tend to tighten their budgets and reduce discretionary spending due to economic uncertainties and job insecurities.

Overall, an economic contraction represents a challenging period marked by reduced production, higher unemployment rates, declining wages, and decreased consumer spending, reflecting the downward phase of the business cycle towards a trough.

3. Peak

During this phase, the economy attains its highest possible rate of expansion. There is a threshold beyond which businesses may be unable to increase production and supply in response to soaring consumer demand. Certain businesses may determine that expanding their production capabilities requires additional investment or expenditure. Additionally, there is a possibility that companies will incur greater production expenses (including wages), which may lead some to pass these costs on to customers in the form of increased pricing.

Despite charging higher prices, companies may consequently experience a "saturation" in profits. Profits for other companies will decline as a result of increased manufacturing (input) expenses or wage demands. In general, inflationary pressures, or "bubbles," begin to accumulate, and the economy overheats. Typically, to cool the economy, the Federal Reserve will increase interest rates to counteract growing prices by increasing the cost of borrowing money.

4. Trough / Depression

Depression, a severe phase of the business cycle, is characterized by a significant slowdown in economic activities. During this period, the growth rate turns negative, leading to a rapid decline in national income and expenditure. Demand for goods and services plummets, prices hit their lowest levels, and businesses are forced to close down production facilities. The rise in unemployment due to workforce reductions results in decreased consumer spending. A notable aspect of depression is the decrease in interest rates, which prompts individuals to hold more cash. Despite lower interest rates, the demand for credit diminishes as investor confidence wanes. Additionally, credit availability may decrease during financial crises. Industries, particularly those producing capital and consumer durable goods, face overcapacity issues. Bankruptcies and liquidations become common, impacting trade and commerce significantly. At the peak of depression, economic activities hit rock bottom, marking the trough phase. The Great Depression of 1929-33 stands as a stark example of the immense suffering and hardship caused by such economic downturns.

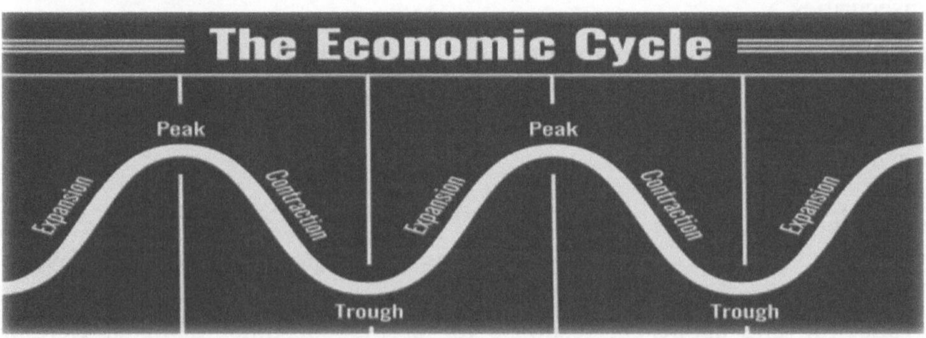

5. Recovery

The economic cycle is a dynamic process that transitions between periods of expansion and contraction, with the lowest point of economic activity known as the trough[2].

The trough signifies the end of pessimism and the beginning of optimism, leading to a reversal in economic trends. Initially, this reversal is evident in the labour market, where widespread unemployment compels workers to accept lower wages.

As business confidence improves, investments increase, stocks are built, and the banking system expands credit. Technological advancements drive fresh investments in machinery and capital goods, leading to increased employment, rising aggregate demand, and gradual price increases.

The upsurge in investment triggers economic recovery, marking a shift from depression to expansion.

With rising investment, production levels increase, employment opportunities grow, incomes rise, and consumer spending begins to climb. The heightened spending boosts aggregate demand, prompting an increase in the production of goods and services. As labour employment rises and unemployment declines, economic activity expands.

It is important to note that economic cycles are not uniform; they vary in intensity and duration, with no fixed pattern to follow. Some cycles may experience prolonged periods of prosperity, while others may linger in depression. Predicting the exact turning points of business cycles remains challenging due to their unpredictable nature and varying characteristics.

Examples of Economic Cycles

1. Great Depression of 1930
2. Information Technology Bubble Burst of 2000
3. Global Economic Crisis (2008-2009)

Features of Business Cycles

The intensity and duration of various business cycles vary. Although they do share certain characteristics, however: Although not with the same degree of regularity, business cycles do transpire at regular intervals. Variable is the duration of each cycle. Additionally, fluctuations differ in intensity[2].

The phases of a business cycle are expansion, apex, contraction, and trough. It is uncommon for these phases to exhibit fluidity and regularity. Additionally, the duration of each phase is indeterminate[2].

Free market economies are typically the origin of business cycles. Additionally, they are pervasive. It is effortless for disruptions to spread to all other sectors from one or more sectors.

While business cycles exert an adverse influence on all sectors, certain industries, including those producing durable consumption goods and capital goods, are disproportionately impacted. Additionally, the industrial sector is more susceptible to the detrimental impacts of trade cycles in comparison to the agricultural sector.

Business cycles are highly intricate phenomena that lack consistent characteristics and underlying causes. They result from an assortment of factors. As a result, precise forecasting of trade cycles prior to their manifestation becomes a challenging endeavour.

Virtually every economic variable, including output, employment, investment, consumption, interest, trade, and price levels, experiences the effects of business cycles simultaneously.

Business cycles have a global scope and are contagious. They originate in one nation and proliferate predominantly through trade relations. In the 1930s, for instance, the Great Depression in the United States and Great Britain impacted nearly every nation, particularly the capitalist nations of the globe.

How to measure it?

Business cycles are measured using various economic indicators, such as[3]:

1. **Gross Domestic Product (GDP)**: The total value of goods and services produced within a country's borders.
2. **Unemployment Rate:** The percentage of the labour force that is without a job but actively seeking employment.
3. **Industrial Production:** A measure of the output of factories, mines, and utilities.
4. **Retail Sales:** A measure of the total value of sales at the retail level.
5. **Consumer Price Index (CPI):** A measure of the average change over time in the prices paid by consumers for a basket of goods and services.
6. **Housing Starts:** A measure of the number of new homes being built.
7. **Stock Market Indicators:** Changes in stock market indices such as the S&P 500 or the Dow Jones Industrial Average can also be used to track business cycles.

Causes of Economic Cycle

Economic cycles are shaped by various internal and external factors.

1. Internal Causes

- Fluctuations in Effective Demand
- Fluctuations in investment
- Variations in government spending
- Macroeconomic policies
- Money Supply
- Psychological factors

2. External Causes

- Wars
- Post War Reconstruction
- Technology shocks
- Natural Factors
- Population growth

How it affects business decisions?

Business decisions may be significantly impacted by business cycles. A comprehensive understanding of the economic climate during the business cycle enables organizations to make well-informed choices regarding production, employment, and investment. Businesses may increase investment in new initiatives, expand their operations, and hire more personnel, for instance, during an expansionary phase. On the contrary, during an economic downturn, enterprises might curtail expenditures, halt production, and implement workforce reductions. Additionally, businesses may modify their pricing strategies in response to economic conditions, such as reducing prices to maintain sales during a recession. Enterprises can enhance their competitiveness, growth rate, and likelihood of success by cultivating an understanding of the business cycle, which enables them to make more informed decisions[3]. Four primary factors influence changes in the business cycle: external issues, business decisions, interest rates, and consumer expectations. Enterprises that increase production capacity thereby augment the aggregate supply thereby contributing to an expansion. When they reduce production, there is a corresponding decrease in supply, which may result in a contraction. An increase in interest rates discourages both businesses and consumers from borrowing funds for purchases, thereby impeding economic growth. A reduction in interest rates enhances the affordability of loans and augments the probability of an economic expansion. Public sentiment toward the condition of the economy exerts an impact on consumer spending, a significant catalyst for aggregate demand. On occasion, external variables, such as international conflicts or natural disasters, may exert an influence on the aggregate supply[3].

Conclusion

In conclusion, the economic cycle, or business cycle, represents the dynamic pattern of economic activity that influences various aspects of a nation's economy. Through its phases of expansion, peak, contraction, and trough, the cycle impacts critical indicators like GDP, employment, and consumer spending. Understanding these phases is essential for investors, businesses, and policymakers to make informed decisions. Historical events, such as the Great Depression and recent crises, serve as reminders of the cycle's impact and the importance of effective management during economic downturns. Internal factors like demand fluctuations and external factors like wars play significant roles in shaping these cycles. Businesses must adapt their strategies, including production, investment, and pricing, to the prevailing economic conditions. Moreover, factors like interest rates and consumer sentiment further influence economic trends. By comprehending these dynamics, stakeholders can navigate the complexities of the economic cycle and position themselves for success in a constantly evolving economic landscape.

References

Reserve Bank of Australia Retrieved from: https://www.rba.gov.au/education/resources/presentations/pdf/the-business-cycle.pdf

Taxman (2024). Business Cycle – Deciphering the Phases. Retrieved from https://www.taxmann.com/post/blog/business-cycle-deciphering-the-phases-causes-and-impacts-for-informed-decision-making.

Vytenis (2023) Importance of business cycles and how it affects business decisions. Retrieved from https://islucid.com/importance-of-business-cycles-and-how-it-affects-business-decisions.

13

The Economics of Subsidies Balancing Support and Sustainability

Diksha Bohra, Narendra Yadav and Aakash Mhaskey

Maharana Pratap University of Agriculture & Technology, Udaipur, Rajasthan

Abstract

The economics of subsidies involve balancing support and sustainability by strategically allocating financial aid to promote environmentally friendly practices and industries. Subsidies play a crucial role in encouraging low-carbon initiatives, renewable energy adoption, and sustainable development. Governments worldwide utilize subsidies to incentivize businesses and consumers to engage in eco-friendly behaviours. For instance, the UK introduced a climate change levy system that allocated subsidies to promote a low-carbon economy, resulting in a significant reduction in carbon emissions. Similarly, countries like Canada, Denmark, the US, and China have implemented various subsidy programs to support renewable energy, energy-saving technologies, and eco-friendly practices.

Introduction

Over the course of past decades India is one of the fastest growing economies of the world with a robust growth and transformations in its economy. In this journey subsidies played a crucial role in influencing market behaviour, support industries, address market failures, and achieve social and economic objectives of the country. Now what actually the economic subsidies are-

Subsidies are financial incentives provided by governments to individuals, businesses, or industries in the form of cash, grants, or tax breaks to influence economic behaviour and outcomes. They aim to correct market failures, promote specific industries, encourage production, and address economic challenges. Subsidies can be direct (cash payments) or indirect (tax breaks), benefiting recipients by reducing burdens or promoting certain actions. They are in the public interest, supporting social goods or economic policies.

The importance of subsidies lies in their ability to offset market failures and externalities, leading to greater economic efficiency. By providing financial aid, subsidies can stimulate production, increase supply, lower prices for consumers, and drive economic growth in targeted sectors. They play a crucial role in stabilizing economies, responding to economic shocks, and promoting long-term economic stability. Subsidies can also help governments address poverty, encourage investment in research and development, and support essential industries like agriculture, energy, and healthcare.

However, the subsidies benefit both the people as well as the economy but only when they are clear, precisely targeted, and appropriately crafted for real-world use, their helpful potential is maximized. The Green Revolution is one instance of how long-term subsidies influences the economy. Good grade grain was provided to farmers at discounted costs. Similarly, we may observe that the Indian government is attempting to lower air pollution through subsidising LPG.

Like indirect taxes, they can change budgetary restrictions and relative prices, which can have an impact on choices about resource allocation, production, and consumption. Sometimes the benefits of subsidies in fields like health, education, and the environment can be justified by pointing out that they help the entire population—past, present, and future—rather than just the immediate beneficiary. However, the situation is less clear-cut for numerous other subsidies. Owing to the government's widespread involvement in a range of economic endeavours, numerous subsidies exist that conceal inefficiencies or have questionable distributional merits. Weaning out of ineffective or distorting subsidies is necessary because their unchecked, unmanaged, and opaque expansion can be detrimental to a nation's public finances.

Overview of the Current Scenario of Subsidies in India

Subsidies currently make up a considerable portion of government spending in India and other countries, even though, like an iceberg, their top may only be visible. As previously mentioned, these implicit subsidies may fail on the altars of equality and efficiency in addition to placing a significant burden on the already stretched fiscal resources.

Subsidies, by means of creating a wedge between consumer prices and producer costs, lead to changes in demand/ supply decisions. Subsidies are often aimed at:

1. Inducing higher consumption/ production
2. Offsetting market imperfections including internalisation of externalities;
3. Achievement of social policy objectives including redistribution of income, population control, etc.

Role of Subsidies in An Economy

The primary reasons why governments give subsidies include:

- **Promoting Economic Stability:** Subsidies are used to stabilize the economy during economic downturns or crises, such as the COVID-19 pandemic. By providing financial aid to individuals and households, subsidies help maintain economic stability and ensure access to essential goods and services.
- **Correcting Market Failures:** Subsidies address market failures by incentivizing activities that have positive externalities or by supporting industries that may not be profitable but are socially beneficial. They can encourage production, consumption, or investment in areas that benefit society.
- **Encouraging Development and Innovation:** Governments use subsidies to promote development in specific sectors, encourage innovation, and boost economic growth. For example, subsidies for research and development (R&D) can stimulate technological advancements and enhance competitiveness.
- **Supporting Essential Industries:** Subsidies are provided to support vital industries like agriculture, healthcare, and energy. By offering financial assistance, governments ensure the sustainability and growth of key sectors that are crucial for the well-being of the population.
- **Addressing Market Imperfections:** Subsidies are used to correct market imperfections, such as inadequate provision of public goods, income inequality, or environmental degradation. They help bridge gaps in the market and promote more efficient resource allocation.
- **Promoting Equity and Social Welfare:** Subsidies play a role in promoting equity by assisting disadvantaged groups or regions. They can help reduce poverty, improve access to essential services, and enhance social welfare by ensuring that basic needs are met for all citizens.
- **Encouraging Export and Trade:** Governments provide export subsidies to support industries that contribute to the country's balance of payments. By incentivizing exports, subsidies can boost international trade and enhance economic competitiveness.

Economic Effects of Subsidies can be Broadly Grouped Into

1. **Allocative effects:** these relate to the sectoral allocation of resources. Subsidies help draw more resources towards the subsidised sector.
2. **Redistributive effects:** these generally depend upon the elasticities of demands of the relevant groups for the subsidised good as well as the

elasticity of supply of the same good and the mode of administering the subsidy.

3. **Fiscal effects:** subsidies have obvious fiscal effects since a large part of subsidies emanate from the budget. They directly increase fiscal deficits. Subsidies may also indirectly affect the budget adversely by drawing resources away from tax-yielding sectors towards sectors that may have a low tax-revenue potential.
4. **Trade effects:** a regulated price, which is substantially lower than the market clearing price, may reduce domestic supply and lead to an increase in imports. On the other hand, subsidies to domestic producers may enable them to offer internationally competitive prices, reducing imports or raising exports.

Additionally, subsidies may have unforeseen or negative economic repercussions. If enforced in a market that is not competitive or in situations where market imperfections do not warrant a subsidy, they would result in an inefficient allocation of resources since they would take funds away from places where their marginal productivity would be higher. In addition to wasting resources, generalized subsidies may have unfavourable distributional effects that benefit the wealthier population more than others. A price control, for instance, may result in decreased production and shortages, which would create black markets. In these markets, operators would profit, and privileged individuals would receive economic rents from the distribution of the good in question at the controlled price.

Negative Impacts of Subsidies

- **Market Distortions:** Subsidies can lead to market distortions by diverting economic resources away from areas where their productivity would be higher, resulting in inefficient resource allocation.
- **Inefficiency and Misallocation:** Some subsidies are considered regressive, poorly targeted, and induce waste and misallocation of resources, leading to inefficiencies in the economy.
- **Dependency:** Excessive reliance on subsidies can create dangerous dependence among various sectors of the economy, hindering growth and innovation.

Concerns Related to Sustainability

- The interconnected concerns of water and energy use in the agricultural sector provide an example of possible environmental or sustainability challenges resulting from the current subsidy structure. India's agricultural output increased significantly during the Green Revolution in the 1960s and 70s, partly because of a sharp rise in agricultural irrigation, especially from groundwater sources. Although the country has been able to feed itself thanks to the expansion of irrigation, this has also brought about a groundwater issue, the extent of which has been made evident in recent years.

- In several sections of the nation, groundwater tables are declining; in Punjab, this is about 20 cm year, while in portions of Gujarat, it might reach 3 to 5 meters annually. In such a situation, the medium- to long-term dangers to agriculture include the entry of saltwater in coastal areas and the eventual loss in water resources. The quantity of electricity needed to pump groundwater from ever-deeper wells rises in tandem with the decline in groundwater tables. Farmers are not motivated to implement water-saving practices because electricity for agriculture is subsidized, which leads to a vicious cycle of excessive water and energy use. The Gujarati government has launched a pilot project to test strategies for encouraging farmers to use more energy- and water-efficient equipment and methods. To encourage the usage of energy, three projects are being carried out in the BESCOM and HESCOM districts of Karnataka under the AgDSM program, or Agricultural Demand Side Management with an objective to promote use of energy efficient pump sets in the irrigation.

Utilisation of Subsidies in Promoting Sustainable food Industry

By allocating financial resources toward eco-friendly procedures and building a more sustainable food system, subsidies can be used to advance sustainability in the food sector. Governments can support smaller farmers, promote the use of sustainable agricultural practices, and stimulate the production of healthier, plant-based diets by repurposing subsidies. Redirecting subsidies in this way can assist in addressing problems including pollution, greenhouse gas emissions, and the use of unsustainable farming practices in the food business.

A crucial tactic is to tie agricultural financial assistance to the preservation of natural areas such as forests. For instance, governments might encourage the preservation of important ecosystems by associating low-cost agricultural loans with farms and municipalities that actively reduce deforestation. This strategy encourages sustainable farming practices by coordinating efforts to enhance food production with programs to save natural resources.

Additionally, supporting integrated programs that bring scientists and producers together can improve conservation efforts related to sustainability. Subsidies can stimulate innovation and lessen the negative environmental effects of food production by funding initiatives that emphasize carbon sequestration, biodiversity conservation, and sustainable agricultural methods.

Furthermore, financial assistance for sustainable operations can be directed by establishing explicit criteria for subsidies and conditioning financing on environmental behaviours. Subsidies can effectively encourage good change in the food business by establishing criteria that prioritize conservation efforts, eco-friendly technologies, and resource efficiency.

All things considered, governments can make a big difference in encouraging environmental stewardship, cutting greenhouse gas emissions, and building a more sustainable future for the food business by carefully rerouting agricultural subsidies toward sustainable methods.

Initiatives and Endorsements which Government can Enforce to Create Environment Sustainability and Current Scenario

Government Subsidies on the Low-Carbon Supply Chain Based on Carbon Emission Reduction Level

The government has changed its approach from subsidising low-carbon products (LCP) to low-carbon technologies to improve low-carbon technology. Game theory is used to model the provision of government subsidies to low-carbon firms and retailers to analyse the effects of these subsidies, which are based on carbon emission reduction levels, on various entities in the low-carbon supply chain (LCSC). The paper's major conclusions are that low-carbon businesses can be effectively incentivized to reduce their carbon emissions by using a government subsidy method depending on degrees of carbon emission reduction. The retail price per unit of low-carbon items, their sales volume, and their revenue per unit are all impacted by the government's choice of subsidy.

The lowest wholesale price per unit for low-carbon products is achieved when the retailer receives government subsidies. In other words, low-carbon businesses raise the wholesale cost of their products to partially offset the cost of government subsidies. While the sales volume and income of low-carbon items are higher in the centralised decision-making framework, the retail price per unit of low-carbon products is lower in the decentralised decision-making framework. The decentralised decision model might be able to make the same amount of money as the centralised decision model thanks to the cost-benefit-sharing agreement.

Subsidising Green Technology

The current state of renewable energy subsidies in India reflects a shift towards supporting renewable sources over fossil fuels, although challenges persist. India has demonstrated its commitment to renewable energy by raising its renewable energy subsidies to Rs 14,843 crore, an increase of 8% from FY 2022. Even though the government has shown a shift in favour of subsidising renewable energy sources rather than fossil fuels, fossil fuel subsidies still outweigh those for renewables, with coal alone receiving more subsidies than renewables. By artificially lowering the cost of coal-fired power, this imbalance can impede the development of renewable energy sources and increase carbon emissions and air pollution. Notwithstanding advancements, ongoing assessment and targeting of subsidies is necessary to guarantee successful results, particularly in terms of expanding access to sustainable energy.

- In addition, the Indian federal and state governments provide financial assistance to private citizens who build solar rooftop systems. To encourage the use of solar energy, the central government offers a 30% rooftop installation subsidy. There are various state-specific subsidy programmes, with differing percentages and qualifying requirements, to promote the installation of solar panels which includes states like Uttar Pradesh, Kerala, Maharashtra, West Bengal, Bihar, and Haryana.
- In the context of fisheries subsidies, the World Trade Organization (WTO) is working towards an ambitious agreement to combat overfishing, biodiversity loss, and CO2 emissions. The agreement aims to prohibit harmful subsidies that drive overfishing and excessive fishing capacity, emphasizing the importance of sustainable practices in the fishing industry. By eliminating subsidies that contribute to overfishing, countries can rebuild fish populations, reduce carbon emissions, and enhance the sustainability of marine resources.

Conclusion

To ensure the effectiveness of subsidies, it is essential to align them with sustainability goals and industry characteristics. Complying with industry norms and environmental objectives is crucial for ensuring the efficacy of subsidies. One strategic way to promote sustainability while managing budgetary demands is to move towards subsidies based on levels of carbon emission reduction, as is the case in China.

A growing emphasis on clean transportation technology and sustainable energy sources is reflected in India's recent increase in subsidies for renewable energy and electric automobiles. The difficulty, though, is in making sure that subsidies are directed appropriately and that a shift to clean energy is backed by precise investment strategies and intermediate goals. The government can lower the societal costs linked to fossil fuels and create a more economical and environmentally friendly energy system in India by strategically allocating energy income to support the shift to renewable energy. By investing in clean energy technologies and promoting sustainable economic growth, India can reinforce its position as a global climate leader and drive a successful energy transition towards a more sustainable future.

Overall, the economics of subsidies require a delicate balance between providing financial support to drive sustainable practices and ensuring that subsidies are effectively targeted to achieve environmental goals. By aligning subsidies with sustainability objectives, governments and organizations can foster a transition towards a greener and more sustainable economy.

References

Helsink, 2006. Retrieved from https://www.oecd.org/fr/croissanceverte/36910476.pdf

Heyl, 2022. Potentials and Limitations of Subsidies in Sustainability Governance: The Example of Agriculture. Sustainability, 14(23), 15859.

Index

A
Animal Husbandry 9, 151
Adequacy 17, 26, 27, 95, 107
Avert 86

B
Bedrock 1, 74, 98
Brokerage 17, 23, 24, 26
Budget 8, 39, 43, 45, 54, 57, 60, 68
Business Cycle 135, 136, 137, 138, 139, 140, 141, 142

C
Crop Diversification 8, 59
Cost Benefit Analysis 10, 11
Crop Insurance 12, 58, 59
Corporate tax 43, 66, 68, 69
Contraction 63, 68, 73, 113, 124, 135, 136, 137, 139, 140, 142

D
Dismantling 42, 45, 52
Depression 91, 135, 136, 138, 139, 140, 142

E
Equity 5, 10, 11, 13, 15, 17, 18, 21, 23, 37, 42, 44, 45, 46, 49, 66, 67, 69, 70, 107, 129, 145
Econometric models 6
Extensive farming 8
Entrepreneurship 21, 72, 92, 93, 98
Economic Reform 37, 38, 39, 40, 52, 109
Environmental 8, 30, 31, 32, 44, 45, 52, 57, 60, 63, 65, 69, 72, 81, 90, 96, 97, 106, 110, 143, 146, 148, 149, 150
Expansion 2, 15, 16, 18, 21, 26, 31, 34, 38, 41, 42, 45, 46, 50, 51, 63, 67, 68, 73, 84, 91, 107, 110, 113, 122, 124, 131, 133, 135, 136, 137, 139, 140, 141, 142, 144, 147

F
Farmer lobbying 8
Fiscal Policy 8, 63, 64, 65, 66, 67, 68, 70, 71, 77
Farmer Producer Organization 11, 59

G
Green Revolution 30, 144, 147
Global Market 1, 5, 30, 48, 49, 57, 65, 106
Globalization 37, 38, 48, 49, 50, 51, 52, 91, 94, 101, 110, 111

H
Hedging 21, 22, 59, 107, 108
Higher Earner 64

I
Inflation 7, 38, 39, 40, 51, 56, 63, 64, 65, 67, 68, 70, 71, 73, 79, 102, 104, 109, 113, 114, 118, 120, 131, 124, 125, 135, 138
Income Redistribution 9, 78

J
Jobs 64, 71, 92, 93, 132, 137

L
Liberalisation 40, 41, 42
Liquor 82

M
Market Stabilization 4, 53, 55
Monoculture Trend 8
Mitigate 12, 15, 17, 22, 26, 37, 58, 59, 68, 72, 95, 103, 114
Market force 3, 4, 30, 34, 37, 53, 54, 55, 56, 57, 59, 60, 103

N
Navigating 63, 64, 65, 72, 74, 98
Non-Tax Revenue 77, 80, 81, 82

O
Open Competition 47
Outsourcing 49
Output 29, 31, 32, 33, 34, 54, 136, 137, 140, 141, 147

P
Price floor 3, 4, 11, 53, 54
Price Smoothing 4
Producer behaviour 5, 8
Price Distortion 9
Privatization 37, 38, 46, 47, 48, 50, 51, 52

Q
Quantity 55, 117, 147
Quantitative 45, 74, 113, 119, 124

R
Reliability 6, 55
Remunerative Prices 7, 54
Risk Management 12, 13, 15, 17, 19, 21, 22, 24, 25, 26, 27, 58, 59, 89, 90, 91, 93, 95, 107, 130
Rigidities 40
Revenue 32, 34, 43, 47, 64, 66, 68, 77, 78, 79, 80, 81, 82, 84, 85, 86, 109, 128, 146, 148
Recovery 48, 135, 139

S
Sustainability 3, 5, 8, 11, 30, 31, 34, 44, 57, 63, 64, 65, 66, 69, 70, 84, 86, 101, 106, 109, 111, 143, 145, 146, 147, 148, 149, 150
Subsidies 7, 8, 12, 31, 32, 71, 143, 144, 145, 146, 147, 148, 149, 150
Subsidized crop 9
SWAP 22, 97, 107
Stakeholder 34, 58, 60, 90, 95, 97, 99, 101, 132, 135, 142
Structural Reform 38, 39, 40

T
Time series 6
Tariff 7, 45, 48, 49, 57, 71, 78, 82
Treasury Bills 17, 20, 22, 26, 115
Tax 31, 39, 40, 43, 44, 49, 63, 64, 65, 66, 67, 68, 69, 71, 77, 78, 80, 81, 82, 84, 86, 96, 116, 128, 129, 143, 144, 146

U
Unpredictable 2, 139
Unveiling 1

V
Vulnerable 1, 2, 9, 10, 93
Volatile 2, 3, 17
Viability 3, 4, 8, 9, 31, 70